Get
Published

The Only Writing Series
You'll Ever Need

Get Published

MEG SCHNEIDER & BARBARA DOYEN

adamsmedia

avon, massachusetts

Copyright © 2008 by F+W Publications, Inc.
All rights reserved.
This book, or parts thereof, may not be reproduced in any
form without permission from the publisher; exceptions are
made for brief excerpts used in published reviews.

Published by
Adams Media, an F+W Publications Company
57 Littlefield Street, Avon, MA 02322. U.S.A.
www.adamsmedia.com

Contains material adopted and abridged from
The Everything® Get Published Book, 2nd Edition
by Meg Schneider and Barbara Doyen,
Copyright © 2006 by F+W Publications, Inc.

ISBN-10: 1-59869-687-4
ISBN-13: 978-1-59869-687-5

Printed in the United States of America.

J I H G F E D C B A

Library of Congress Cataloging-in-Publication Data
is available from the publisher.

This book is available at quantity discounts for bulk purchases.
For information, please call 1-800-289-0963.

Contents

Introduction

This is *The Only Writing Series You'll Ever Need: Get Published.* That's a big promise! But it can happen—if you follow the advice in this simple and straightforward book, you will find that getting published is actually possible.

It's true, there has always been a certain romance about writers and writing—but along with the glamorous notion of the industry comes the serious mystery of *how does it all actually happen?*

How do people get their ideas to write? How do they know if they are good enough to be published? And how do they get an agent and actually, finally, get their work out there? In the end, most published writers feel like their energy, time, and work was well worth it. So how did they do it? And how can you? It's easy!

Whether you are a beginner writer who is just experimenting and honing a hobby or you've been writing for years and you're sick of receiving rejection letters, this book will act as your cheat sheet to success. Exposing the truths of the publishing industry as well as suggesting ways to get past common writer's roadblocks, this experienced agent and author team will take the mystery out of making your work marketable.

If you're considering sending clips to a newspaper or magazine, interested to try your hand a book proposal, or simply want to get your work up on the Internet, let this book guide you along the often-times meandering path that is the publishing industry.

What are you waiting for?

Chapter 1

Welcome to the World of Publishing

Newspapers

Your local newspaper can be a great training ground for developing your freelance career. Aside from the opportunity to hone your writing skills and learn how to work with an editor, it's a good place to develop story ideas for other markets. A story about an innovative new business in your community might be of interest (with the proper slant) to a larger newspaper, a regional magazine, or a trade journal, and, through the story for the local paper, you've already done some of the research and developed some sources.

Opinion Pages

Letters to the editor and guest opinion essays are excellent openings for beginning writers. You won't get paid for them, but you will get authorship credit, and these short pieces are valuable exercises because they force you to tighten and clarify your writing. Most local newspapers have a limit of 250 words for letters to the editors, and perhaps 600 to 800 words for guest essays. You don't have room for excessive exposition here; you have to make the most effective use of your limited space.

Helpful Hints

It's harder to get your letter to the editor or opinion piece published by larger newspapers. *The New York Times*, for example, receives thousands of letters each week, and only a very select few ever get published. Those that do are generally quite short—100 words or fewer.

Some newspapers have policies limiting how many times you can have a letter or opinion piece published. They might publish a letter from you only once every thirty days, for example. Longer pieces will be published even less often, unless the paper asks you to write a regular column. If that happens, you might well be offered a small honorarium for your contribution, and you may be asked to commit to writing your column for six months or a year.

Weekly newspapers and small dailies often are more open to accepting regular columns from contributing writers (that is, writers who aren't on the newspaper's staff). Pay for your services will be minimal, but a well-written and well-read column can be a springboard to other writing opportunities.

Food, Entertainment, and Travel

Medium- and large-circulation newspapers usually have sections devoted to food, entertainment, travel, and other special interests, such as hobbies. Often these newspapers accept articles from freelancers for these sections, especially if they don't have staff reporters who are interested or available to cover these beats. Again, pay usually is low, but you generally get a byline and clips to add to your portfolio.

For food sections, you might be able to review new restaurants, interview chefs in your area, or even write a feature on unusual items for the barbecue or cool new kitchen gadgets. Entertainment sections usually cover such things as movies and concerts but also extend to articles on exhibits and lectures at area art and science museums, festivals, and maybe even architecture and local history. Travel sections usually use wire services such as AP or Reuters for major domestic and international destinations, but there may be opportunities for you to highlight local attractions.

Become a Stringer

Occasional submissions to a local newspaper can turn into a regular freelance gig. Stringers, as they are known in the business, are basically on-call reporters who are assigned articles when the regular staff of reporters is too busy to do them. Depending on your newspaper's coverage area, it may need stringers to cover high school sports, graduations, or other events where there are too many things for one person to cover. Some newspapers have general-assignment stringers who aren't limited to any one beat or particular area of coverage. Some have stringers who cover only sports, business, or other specific beats. Pay rates for stringers vary widely and may be based on so much per article or column inch, or on hours worked.

Magazines

As exciting and gratifying as it is to see your byline in *Cosmo* or *GQ*, the truth is that these large markets are highly competitive and almost always out of reach for beginners. However, there are hundreds of smaller magazines, many of which welcome new writers. Pay rates and circulations often are lower than with the big national magazines, but a solid track record with them can help open doors down the road.

Trade Journals

Virtually every sector of business has its own magazine, and very often there are several magazines covering various aspects of a particular industry. These highly focused magazines are known as trade journals, and they have very specialized needs for very specialized readerships. *Northeast Export*, for example, covers New England's international trade community. The *Chief of Police* magazine is targeted to the command ranks of law enforcement agencies. There are hundreds more; *Writer's Market* devotes nearly 150 pages just to paying trade journal markets.

Trade journals are always looking for well-written articles that meet the needs of their readers, and they are generally open to beginning writers, as long as you can supply appropriate material. This doesn't mean you have to be an expert, or even a practitioner, in the field, but you do have to be able to write for a knowledgeable reader. If you have lots of good ideas for a trade area that interests you, you can make a respectable income while you build a collection of clips.

Helpful Hints

One of the easiest ways to break into the trade journals is to examine the magazines in your own profession, or that of someone close to you, such as a parent, spouse, or friend. As with any potential market, study several issues of a journal to get a feel for the kinds of information it publishes and the writing style.

Consumer Magazines

Most people think of the big national magazines that you see at supermarket checkouts and bookstores when they think of consumer magazines. As noted earlier, these can be hard to break into. But there are hundreds of smaller consumer magazines. Some of them have a general-interest slant, but many of them fill narrower niches, such as rock-climbing, star-gazing, gourmet cooking, or home decorating. If you have a hobby, chances are there's a consumer magazine that could be interested in your material.

Starting out with small consumer magazines can give you the credentials you'll probably need to break into the larger publications. Even so, when you're first starting to approach the big magazines, you have a better chance of breaking in with shorter pieces. The big national magazines generally reserve their main features for established writers, but they also usually have departments that are open to newcomers.

The Internet

The Internet has given rise to a whole new world of potential markets for writers. Every Web site must have content, and Web site operators often need writers to supply that content. If you connect with the right place and know how to write effectively for the Web, you can command respectable fees for your work.

Writing for the Web

According to various studies, Internet users are an impatient bunch. They are willing to wait an average of eight seconds for a Web page to load; if it takes longer, they give up and go somewhere else. They generally like small nuggets of information and tend to shy away from text-heavy pages that scroll on forever. If they can't find what they're looking for within a few seconds on a given page, they try another site.

Most of these issues can be resolved in the design of a Web page. But an effective design requires effective structure in the content. Long pieces generally should be broken into sections to allow for easier navigation. Links to additional information often need to be imbedded in the text. Writers need to think about the keywords users will search for to find what they want.

Helpful Hints

Whenever you post your writings on the Web, whether it's through an e-zine, a blog, or on your own site, it counts as publication. If you post an essay about your cat, for example, you can't sell first serial rights to that same essay to Cat Fancy magazine; the best you can offer is second serial rights.

Writing for the Web can be a challenge, especially for writers who aren't accustomed to thinking about space limitations. It requires tightly focused text, an understanding of how readers will use the site, and insight into what readers want and need. If you can master these elements, you can make a name for yourself creating content for any number of businesses and organizations that need a continual supply of fresh material for their sites.

"Guide" Sites

Becoming an expert guide on sites like About.com can provide a big boost for your writing career. It gives you a platform for marketing magazine articles and book proposals, especially if your articles and book ideas are related to your guide topic. Writing regularly for these sites helps you sharpen your skills, and many such sites pay respectable fees to their guides.

The field is fairly competitive, and the more well-known guide sites have a fairly rigorous screening process for hiring guides. These sites also require you to commit your time to research and writing, because you'll be expected to provide regular updates to your page. However, as in any aspect of publishing, there are other ways to break in. For example, Amazon.com allows you to put together a virtual reference library on a topic you're interested in. You won't get paid for this, but you will draw in other readers who share your interest, and a comprehensive resource list under your name helps establish you as an expert on your topic.

Things to Consider

If you get a contract to write Web site content, go over the provisions carefully. It's reasonable for the site owner to prohibit you from putting material you've written for the Web site into a book. However, the contract should not prohibit you from writing any print books on any topic related to the content you create for the site. Such a requirement is overly broad and even unnecessary, since the target markets for Web sites and print books usually are significantly different.

Helpful Hints

Articles you write for Web sites often are work-for-hire arrangements. That means you get paid for what you write, but the site owner keeps all rights to the article; you can't sell reprint rights, for example. This usually isn't of too much concern, because most publications aren't interested in printing something that already has appeared on the Internet to a global audience.

Your contract also might bar you from providing any articles, on any topic, to competing Web sites unless you get prior approval from the site you're contracting with. This also is a reasonable demand, but, again, make sure it isn't too broad. If you've contracted with a food Web site, you should be free to contribute articles to time-management Web sites, for example.

Payment for Web content might be calculated in the form of a flat fee or, more often, as a percentage of advertising revenue based on page viewership. Some writers don't like the percentage arrangement because they don't get paid up front for their work. In practice, though, this payment method is like receiving royalties on a book; the more people read your work, the more money you make. Site operators like it because they don't pay for content no one reads, and the onus is on the author to provide interesting, relevant, and useful material on a continual basis.

Commercial Opportunities

Businesses and nonprofit organizations need a variety of written materials to support their missions, and they often look to outside agencies or independent contractors to produce these materials for them. The people who write these materials don't usually get a byline, but they are well paid for their skills, and they get nice finished pieces for their portfolios.

Corporate Communications

Businesses may hire you to write annual or quarterly reports for investors, press releases about new products or services, a history of the company, speeches for executives to deliver at stockholder meetings or other events, content for their Web sites, or copy for brochures. Large businesses usually hire professional advertising or public relations agencies to handle these projects, or they may have their own in-house departments. Smaller businesses, which may not be able to afford the retainers agencies charge and may not have the time or expertise to create their own materials, often are delighted to find an individual willing to do the work for a reasonable fee. Nonprofits often have the same financial and expertise restrictions of small businesses. And, many times, these clients are willing to hire writers with little or no experience for these assignments.

Helpful Hints

Some writers will do corporate and nonprofit projects for a flat fee, while others prefer to charge an hourly rate, which can range from $25 to $150 or more. An hourly rate ensures you get paid for additional work if your client asks for substantial changes.

A freelance writer who can effectively communicate an organization's message in a variety of media can make good money and build a reputation for himself. You should be able to write in the client's voice, master the key points the client wants to make, and understand the market the client is trying to reach.

Advertising

Small businesses and nonprofits often can use help writing advertising copy as well. If you can craft an effective message for direct mail campaigns, print or electronic advertising, and even flyers, you have an opportunity to sell those skills to establishments that don't have the time or resources to do it themselves. A flair for phrasing is important, as is an ability to persuade your audience to take action.

Newsletters

Writing a weekly, monthly, or quarterly newsletter can give you a steady income and, over time, expertise on a particular topic. Many companies, even smaller ones, have a regular newsletter for employees; some even have one for their vendors or customers who have signed up on a mailing list. If you have even a basic desktop publishing program on your computer, you can offer your design services as well as your writing talents.

Like any other publication, newsletters usually have a specific mission and a specific audience. An employee newsletter, for instance, is likely to focus on company policies, benefit information, training opportunities, and the like. A newsletter for vendors might include requests for proposals or bids on a company project or discuss how a vendor's product helps the company succeed. One aimed at customers likely will highlight special offers, new products or services, and the company's philosophy.

Helpful Hints

E-zines, or online newsletters, make the cost of producing your own newsletter negligible and allow you to reach a broader audience, which helps you build a platform for other publishing opportunities. Writing an e-zine for stay-at-home mothers with 5,000 subscribers is a hefty credential for the article you want to sell to *Parenting* magazine.

Working on newsletters can help you advance your career, particularly if you're trying to sell articles or books that relate to your newsletter focus. If you can't find one that suits your goals, consider starting your own and build a subscriber base. It can be as broadly or as narrowly tailored as you like, but it should be about something that interests you because you'll be writing about it a lot. Potential topics include hobbies, charitable or political causes, or social issues.

Books

Book publishing is widely seen as the pinnacle of writing success, and there is fierce competition to be one of the "chosen:" a bona fide book author. Even experienced writers with killer clips sometimes have a hard time landing that first book contract. But, like every other market in publishing, there are opportunities for talented writers who do their homework and match their work with the right market.

Adult Fiction

Seventy percent of all books sold in the United States every year are books for adults, and fiction for adults accounts for 50 percent of the American book market. Little wonder, then, that so many aspiring writers dream of being the next Amy Tan, Dan Brown, Stephen King, or Danielle Steel. Besides, fiction is where your imagination and creativity have free rein; for many writers, the fun is in fiction.

Unfortunately, adult fiction is one of the most difficult book markets for new writers to break into, partly because there is so much competition. That doesn't mean there's no room for new talent. On the contrary, agents and editors are always looking for well-written stories with strong characterization and plots that will captivate readers. But if you don't have all those elements in your manuscript, it's difficult to get your fiction noticed.

Researching potential markets is essential for marketing your novel. If you're writing romances, know what romance publishers require. Many of them insist that any explicit sex or violence take place off-stage; some won't consider interracial or interfaith characters; some don't want stories that involve infidelity or premarital sex.

Helpful Hints

The number one complaint from agents and editors is that they receive material that is not appropriate for them. Study the guidelines in the print directories and online to find out whether an element in your story excludes it from a particular market. If it does, don't waste your time—or the agent's or editor's—by submitting it.

New fiction authors almost always have to have their manuscripts completed before they begin marketing. Many agents and editors have been burned by hopeful writers who can't complete an entire novel. You may even be required to finish the manuscript before getting a contract for your second or third novel.

When it is time to market your novel, you need to have a clear idea of who your target readers are. Agents and editors are never impressed by claims that "everyone" will want to read your book. You don't have to provide hard numbers in your marketing package, but you do have to give an agent or editor an idea of where your book will fit on a bookstore shelf. Do this by identifying the genre of your novel and, if appropriate, published authors whose works are similar to yours. You shouldn't claim to be the next Amy Tan, but you can describe your novel as an Italian-American *Joy Luck Club*.

Adult Nonfiction

Fiction writers sometimes turn up their noses at nonfiction opportunities because nonfiction is not what they want to write. But nonfiction is easier for unpublished authors to break into, and a non-fiction book credit is helpful when you market your novel, because you are no longer an untried writer. The main question agents and editors have about new authors is whether they're capable of com-pleting book-length work. Even though styles and demands are dif-ferent in fiction and nonfiction, the fact that you've been published marks you as a professional book author.

Another advantage to nonfiction is that you don't have to write the entire manuscript in order to make a sale. Most sales are made on the basis of a proposal, which describes both your book and the market for it. If you can find a niche to be filled and craft a well-written, well-targeted proposal, you have a good chance of landing a contract.

Children's Books

The children's book market is, in many ways, even more com-petitive than the adult markets. Publishers receive tons of queries and manuscripts for children's books, both fiction and nonfiction, but only a select few ever make it into print. The good news is that the children's market holds great opportunities for talented writers who know how to write for this demanding readership.

Children's book publishers usually define readers by age groups, progressing in stages from infants and toddlers to teens. There's plenty of room for both fiction and nonfiction in the children's market. Advances and royalty rates tend to be lower than for adult fiction and nonfiction, but children's books often stay in print longer, and children often become lifelong fans of their favorite authors.

Chapter 2

Set Yourself Up for Success

Learn the Tools of the Trade

As in any profession, writers need the proper tools to do their work. You may like to write your stories or articles in longhand on a legal pad, or you might like the clacking of the keys of a manual typewriter. But when it comes time to submit your work to agents and editors, you need the equipment that will make you look like a pro.

Computers and the Internet

A handful of professional writers still cling to the old-fashioned typewriter. But the proliferation of relatively inexpensive home computers and cheap Internet access has made such equipment the industry standard for publishing these days. Indeed, so many publishers—of newspapers, magazines, and books—now prefer to receive assigned material electronically that you put yourself at an unnecessary disadvantage if you don't have a home computer and an e-mail account.

Your personal computer doesn't have to be fancy. You need a good word-processing program, a good-quality printer, and a reliable Internet Service Provider, or ISP. The industry standard for word-processing software is Microsoft Word, although some publishers will accept material in other formats. Word is not typically included in the software bundles for most home computers, so you may have to purchase the program separately or upgrade the software package when you buy your computer.

Ink-jet and laser printers deliver a quality hard copy of your material, and they also are fairly inexpensive. Unless you plan to use it for other things, you don't need a color printer. The only acceptable design for submitting your writing is to use black ink on white paper. It is the easiest combination to read and the most professional. Colored inks and papers—even for your letterhead—are hard on the eyes and will immediately brand you as an amateur in the eyes of agents and editors.

Helpful Hints

Incompatible word-processing programs can result in formatting errors and, often, simply lines of gibberish. If you aren't using Microsoft Word, you may have to convert your material to a text-only file when you submit it. This ensures the recipient will be able to open and read the file, regardless of which program either of you is using.

Likewise, your ISP doesn't have to have all the bells and whistles. You need a reliable way to send and receive e-mail and to do Web-based research when warranted. Keep in mind that some ISPs put limits on the size of e-mail attachments, as well as on the amount of server space you have for archiving e-mail.

Office Supplies

Most agents and editors judge materials based on the content, and not necessarily on the way they are presented and packaged. But presentation and packaging can reinforce your image as a professional—or as an amateur. And, in the highly competitive arena of publishing, aspiring writers need every edge they can get.

Start giving yourself that edge by selecting good-quality supplies. Use a 20-pound, white typing paper with some rag or linen content for all your submissions, even your letterhead. For query submissions, use a good-quality, white number 10 business envelope; enclose the same kind of envelope, folded in thirds and paper-clipped to your query letter, as your SASE. For submissions of more than five pages, use a 9 × 12 or 10 × 14 manila mailer; again, enclose the same kind of envelope, folded in half, as your SASE.

Most word-processing programs have a mailing label function, and your submission will look most professional if you use typed address labels. If you must handwrite addresses, use block letters to ensure readability. Remember to include your own address on your SASE.

Helpful Hints

Always print all of your materials—queries, cover letters, proposals, and manuscripts—on one side of the page only. Printing on two sides may save you a few pennies on paper, but it will annoy the agent or editor and make it more difficult for him to read your submission.

Aside from mailing labels, your own handwriting should appear only on the signature line of your query or cover letter. Always sign in pen, never pencil, and use black or blue ink for a professional look. Avoid red ink; studies have shown that people react negatively to red, whether on graded tests in school or in your signature. Other colored inks, like green, purple, or pink, may look whimsical and fun, but they are not appropriate for professional communications.

Your Reference Library

Every writer needs her own reference library. In addition to a good dictionary, a good thesaurus, and a good style guide to resolve grammar and punctuation questions, your library should include an up-to-date directory of potential markets. It may also include inspirational books about the writing life and how-to guides like this one, as well as general references like encyclopedias.

Other titles in your library will depend on what type of writing you do or want to do. If you're writing historical fiction, a guide to the latest scientific discoveries probably won't be of much use to you. On the other hand, a book describing everyday life in the 1800s might be indispensable. No matter what your genre, there are countless books available that can be of help in developing your career.

Finally, your personal reference library should include writer's guidelines and sample issues of the publications you hope to break into. Many magazines include their guidelines on their Web sites, and most will send you a hard copy in exchange for your SASE. Sample issues usually can be ordered for a small fee.

Setting Goals for Yourself

Many aspiring writers talk about what they will do "someday," trusting in luck and inspiration to fulfill their dreams. If you're serious about a writing career, though, you'll benefit from setting realistic short- and long-term goals. The more specific your goals are, the easier it is to identify steps you can take to achieve them, and the more control you have over the direction and progression of your career.

Selecting a Specialty

Especially in fiction, new writers benefit from specializing in one genre. Having several sci-fi short stories published helps give you a platform for marketing your sci-fi novel. And it will be easier to find a publisher for your second novel if it's the same genre as your first; staying with one genre helps build a fan base among readers, and your second book will be more attractive to a publisher if you already have that fan base to tap into.

Helpful Hints

Fiction writers can benefit from adding nonfiction pieces to their clip files. Nonfiction is easier for new writers to break into, giving you those all-important published credits. You also can strengthen your fiction platform if your nonfiction clips are related to your fiction—if your nonfiction is on new scientific discoveries, for example, and your short story is sci-fi.

This doesn't mean you can't jump from one genre to another. But, in most cases, that jump is better delayed until after your second or even third novel is published. Besides, the more experience you gain in getting stories or novels of one genre published, the more confident you will be when it's time to try something different.

Nonfiction writers generally don't have the same restrictions on category, but, like fiction writers, they can get typecast for certain assignments. If your clip file mainly consists of profiles of sports figures, for instance, you might have trouble convincing an editor that you're qualified to write an article about global warming. Some writers get a reputation for delivering quality feature-length articles, and editors are loath to waste these writers' talents on shorter, newsy pieces. That said, it generally is easier for nonfiction writers to get a variety of assignments, giving you a more well-rounded portfolio.

Time Management

Many new writers have difficulty finding the time to focus on their writing. Other obligations—family, your regular job, social engagements, and so on—eat up so much of the day, and so much of your mental energy, that there often isn't any to spare for the creative process. Then, too, beginning writers often don't know where to start work on their project, so they just never get around to it. Here are some tips that other writers have found useful; experiment with them to find a solution that works for you.

- **Make a standing appointment with yourself.** Set aside a block of time (ideally the same time every day) for writing and schedule other obligations around that time.
- **Write at different times of the day.** Experimenting with the time of day can help you discover when you're at your most creative and productive.
- **Set up a place to write.** Even if it's just a corner of the living room, a dedicated place to write can help you focus.
- **Limit your writing time.** This may sound counterintuitive, but having too much time can interfere with getting to work.

- **Set a goal for each day's or each week's work.** Personal deadlines for finishing a chapter, a character bio, a synopsis, or needed research can help keep you motivated and on track.

The challenge for most new writers is making writing a priority among all the other priorities in your life. At the beginning of your career, before you break into the larger markets and begin to see a substantial return on your investment of time and energy, it's all too easy to let your writing slip into hobby status. But that initial investment is essential if your goal is to become a professional writer.

Juggling Projects

Professional writers are masters at juggling various projects, and they almost always have several projects going at once, in various stages of development. There are several advantages to this, not the least of which is the fact that, when you have a second project to work on, you're less likely to obsess over the fate of your first project. There are always new ideas to pursue, which can be a great comfort when one of your ideas doesn't go anywhere.

Helpful Hints

Set up a system to keep track of ideas as they occur to you. It doesn't have to be elaborate; it can be as simple as a set of index cards on which you jot notes about potential stories or articles. If you can make notes about ideas when they occur, then file them away safely, these new ideas are less likely to distract you from your current project.

Writing projects have four main stages of development: the thinking-up stage, the research stage, the query stage, and the writing stage. Ideally, you should have one project in each of these phases at any given time. As soon as you send out a query for one idea, begin doing the research for one of your other ideas. This keeps you busy while you're waiting to hear back on your first query. Once you get a sale, you'll have the full cycle going—writing for the sale, querying your next idea, researching markets or information for a third idea, and dreaming up fourth, fifth, and sixth ideas.

Writing for Free, then Getting Paid

When you're just starting out, you may find that the only markets open to you are ones that pay little or nothing to their contributors. But these markets can help you build the foundation for a more lucrative career. They also can help you build a platform, which makes you more salable to bigger markets. Many publications invite readers to contribute ideas, and most have a letter-to-the-editor feature. For example, *Sew News* has a column of tips provided by readers; if their tip is used, they receive a gift, such as a free subscription. *Better Homes and Gardens* has a letters department; if your letter is published, you do not get paid, but you can claim contributor's credit in the magazine.

Newspapers, of course, have active letters-to-the-editor sections. The bigger the newspaper, the more difficult it is to get your letter printed. However, if you've had two dozen letters to the editor printed in the *New York Times* or the *Los Angeles Times*, that could impress an agent or editor. It even could lead to an invitation to write a longer op-ed piece for pay.

Helpful Hints

Shorter usually is better for letters to the editor, especially for large publications. Speak your mind in a maximum of 150 words, and you'll increase the odds of getting your letter published. Op-ed pieces, also called guest editorials, usually can run between 400 and 800 words, depending on the publication.

Most of the nonpaying markets are small-circulation newspapers and magazines. For some small book publishers, too, you might have to work without an advance, but you should get royalties from sales of your book. A handful of Web sites pay their contributors, but most don't, and the ones that do, like the major publications, are more difficult for newcomers to break into.

The key benefit to you with nonpaying markets is credit, credit, credit. If you don't get a byline, and you don't get paid, then you'll be doing the work for the love of it. There's nothing wrong with that, if that's what you choose. But, for the career-minded writer, the real value of these markets is the opportunity to build your clip file and to use these credits as a springboard to bigger things.

Where Does the Money Come In?

As you gain experience, you'll move into paying markets, and these, too, typically follow a progression from smaller fees to larger ones. Depending on the type of market, your fee might be based on so much per word, so much per printed page, or a flat fee. Flat fees often are quite small, but not always; *Reader's Digest*, for example, pays a flat fee of $300 for its "Life in These United States," "Humor in Uniform," and "All in a Day's Work" features, which run 100 words or fewer. That works out to $3 or more a word—a very good pay rate for writers. Sometimes it's easier to assess the fairness of the pay by converting it to an hourly rate. Twenty-five cents a word may sound like a respectable rate on its face, but if the research is going to take a great deal of time, the pay may not be worth the effort. Balance these factors and others in choosing your projects.

The bigger your portfolio gets, the more leverage you'll have to negotiate better pay rates—and the more confidence you'll have in asking for more money. Remember that the pay rates listed in market directories like *Writer's Market* often are just averages. You might be offered less money than the listing indicates, especially if you're an unknown. On the flip side, you might be offered more if you've proven yourself as a reliable contributor.

Get It in Writing

Writers' Web sites are teeming with horror stories of writers who received assignments and whose work was published, but who never received payment. Having a written agreement is no guarantee that you will get paid, but a publication willing to put the assignment and the fee in writing is more likely to be on the up-and-up. Most professional writers refuse to do any work without a contract.

Especially for magazines, contracts can be quite short and simple. At some publications, the contract consists of a few lines on the back of the payment check; endorsing the check also executes the contract. It should spell out the nature of the assignment—or the title of an already-written article or short story—as well as the fee to be paid and when the writer can expect payment, such as "on acceptance" or "on publication." Because magazines usually have lead times of several months, and because your article or story might get pushed back for a number of reasons, getting paid "on acceptance" is the better option for you.

Helpful Hints

Some writers advocate sending an invoice when you submit articles that have been assigned. If you have a contract for the article, an invoice generally is unnecessary. However, if the arrangements have been made by telephone or e-mail, an invoice that describes the piece and the agreed-upon payment can be a backup for your records.

Saying No

Payment for your articles or short stories should be commensurate with the quality of your clips and the work involved in the current project. If you're like most writers, you may start out working for little or no pay, but once you've paid your dues with smaller markets, you should be able to garner bigger earnings. And once you've written an article or two at twenty-five or fifty cents a word, you should have enough confidence to turn down the markets that only pay ten cents a word, or to insist on an increase in payment.

Writers who stick with it generally grow beyond the small markets that gave them their start, in terms of both profile and pay. You might still do occasional work for a small magazine once you've managed to break into larger markets, and that's fine. But those occasions probably will become rarer as your career builds and the value others place on your work grows.

Building a Credential Pool

Just as your per-word rate should increase as you gain more experience as a published writer, your credential file should follow a natural progression from smaller to larger markets. Little pieces in little markets lead to bigger pieces in those same markets, which lead to small pieces in larger markets, and they in turn lead to longer pieces in the big markets.

The easiest places for most rookie writers to break in usually are in their own backyards. Check out freelance opportunities with your local newspaper or with regional magazines. Local business journals, entertainment magazines, and the like can provide excellent opportunities for beginners. And clips from these kinds of publications can help open doors at larger newspapers and magazines.

Don't neglect trade journals in your quest to capture clips. Company or individual profiles, new products, discoveries in medicine or other sciences—these are just a few likely areas for potential articles. Pay rates in the trades vary widely; in some cases, getting a published credit may be more important than how much you get paid, but some of these journals pay very well for well-researched, well-written articles.

Helpful Hints

Be open to working with the editor at your local newspaper. Especially if you have no formal journalism training, you might have much to learn about how newspaper stories are constructed. A good working relationship with your editor is more likely to lead to additional assignments, as well as a more impressive clip file.

The high-profile national magazines are the most difficult for newcomers to crack, but even these usually offer some opportunities. Think small when you're approaching these markets, at least at first.

Feature-length pieces almost always are reserved for staff writers or for freelancers who have a track record with the editor or the publication. But most magazines have departments at the front or back of the "book" (the industry term for the magazine) that are open to new writers. These pieces usually are shorter and often don't pay as much as features, but they are an excellent way to build a reputation with a particular magazine.

Play by the Rules

New writers can get frustrated by what seem like arcane and foolish rules for breaking into the publishing world. Indeed, from the outside, publishing can seem like a closed circle, admitting only a select few for indeterminate reasons. But the rules that govern the publishing world actually are intended to benefit both writers and the people who make the decisions about what makes it into print.

Submission Guidelines

Agents and editors receive a mind-boggling amount of material every day. Some of it arrives by regular mail, some by delivery services like UPS or FedEx, and an astounding amount by e-mail. And this is just the material from hopeful new writers; it doesn't even count the vast amount of material from established clients and freelancers. Agents and editors establish submission guidelines to cope with the ever-growing mountain of material on their desks.

Helpful Hints

Treat e-mail addresses as the privilege that they are, and don't share them with anyone unless you have the agent's or editor's permission to do so. Most agents and editors still prefer to receive queries and other preliminary submissions by regular mail and reserve e-mail for active projects.

The best thing new writers can do for themselves is follow the submission guidelines listed in the market directories. Doing so demonstrates your respect for the agent's or editor's time and marks you as a professional. Other ways of approach might look like shortcuts, but really they are unnecessary detours.

Match Your Material

If a market doesn't accept personal profiles or humor, you waste your time and theirs by submitting personal profiles and humor. Take the time to research the markets before you send out queries and match your material to markets that are looking for what you write. Publishing can be a maddeningly slow business anyway; don't slow it down further by aiming in the wrong direction.

How Teaching Can Help

Teaching is an excellent way to be regarded as an expert on a topic, and that expertise adds substantial heft to your credentials when it's time to pursue getting published. And, depending on where you live and what kind of venues are available to you, you might not have to go through the rigors of getting a teaching certificate or license.

Community Colleges

Community colleges and even some K–12 school districts often have adult or community education programs. These usually don't count as college credits. They are aimed at personal development and enrichment, with courses in subjects like gardening, auto maintenance, foreign languages, crafts, personal finance, and the like.

Because these classes aren't offered for credit, the requirements for instructors usually are less stringent. If you can come up with a proposal for a class that's likely to appeal to a good number of people and demonstrate some expertise in the topic you're proposing, you might be able to get a gig teaching a for-fun class.

Community education classes usually are scheduled for evenings and weekends to allow the greatest number of working adults to take advantage of them. That means you can teach these courses on the side while still holding down your regular job—and while pursuing your writing.

Another advantage to these courses is that you can structure them to suit you. You can craft a one-day seminar-type class and schedule it for a Saturday or you can design it as a continuing course, meeting for, say, two or three hours on Tuesday evenings for three weeks. Contact your college or school district to find out what their instructor requirements, scheduling preferences, and course needs are.

Interim Courses

Some two- and four-year colleges offer intensive courses between regular semesters; these often are scheduled in January, between the holidays and the beginning of the regular spring semester. Students take one course for two or three weeks, spending several hours a day in this one class. These classes often are given for college credit, so the standards for instruction may be more rigorous. But if you have the right credentials for the course (which are not necessarily the same credentials you need for getting published), interim teaching assignments might provide opportunities for you to bolster your platform.

Online Courses

More and more colleges are turning to the Internet to teach students. It's more convenient for many students, especially adults who are returning to college and have to fit their class work into an already full schedule, and it's often more convenient for instructors, who can do their work and be available for their students without being tied to an office. Sometimes, colleges will hire people with real-life experience in the subject being taught to conduct these online classes; they don't necessarily impose the same requirements for these types of courses as they do on regular faculty positions.

Whatever teaching option you pursue, it's always best if you can relate the topic you're teaching to the topic you want to write about. If you want to write about fine dining, for example, the best courses for you to teach might be ones on gourmet cooking, or wine selection, or preparing an elegant dinner party at home.

Helpful Hints

Even after you've been published, teaching can help bolster your platform. The more published credits you have in a given topic, the more attractive colleges will find you as an instructor. You also might be able to use your published clips, whether articles or books, as teaching aids for your course.

Combining courses and your writing topics can help you get established as a writer, and once you have some clips, it will be easier for you to branch out into other topics and genres.

Conferences and Seminars

If you can't teach through traditional channels, consider getting involved in conferences and seminars. Some cities have speakers' bureaus, which act as a kind of broker to link audiences and presenters. Check with your local chamber of commerce to see if there's such an organization in your area. You also can arrange your own seminars, if you're willing to put in the work. Choose a topic in which you are both interested and well-versed; people who attend conferences and seminars expect to learn something new and useful.

Conference Opportunities

If you have a particular area of expertise—and by that, we mean something more than a hobby—you might be able to give presentations at professional conferences. You can participate in panel discussions, serve as facilitator of a break-out session, or even deliver a keynote speech. The best place to search for such opportunities is through professional associations. If you're a member of the Public Relations Society of America (PRSA), for instance, contact the head of your chapter to find out what kind of conferences are scheduled and what presentations you might be suited to offer.

Even if you aren't a member of an organization, you might be a good candidate for offering a presentation. Maybe a local PRSA conference would be interested in hearing from a television or newspaper reporter about effective ways to pitch stories to the media. If your expertise is in database management, maybe members of your local or state American Medical Association chapter could use your information to improve their record-keeping. Look for ways that your area of expertise can be made useful to specific, targeted audiences.

Helpful Hints

How can you use conferences and seminars to promote your writing? After your presentation, lots of folks will want to talk to you one-on-one. Be sure to exchange business cards; if one of the attendees would be an impressive endorser for your book proposal, you'll have a unique opening to get it.

DIY Seminars

If professional conferences aren't the best fit for you, you might want to explore offering your own seminars. Again, select a topic that you're familiar with and interested in, and make sure your seminar offers value for the attendees. "How To" topics usually generate the most interest: How to Maximize Your Investments, How to Get Started in Real Estate, How to Write a Business Plan, How to Home School Your Children, etc. As we noted in the teaching section, it's best for your writing career if you can design a seminar related to the topic you want to write about.

Conferences and seminars give you a platform for your related writing topic because they show that you know the market for your topic and the needs of your audience or readership. In addition, writers who have a track record of public speaking are considered more promotable, especially by book publishers.

Whole books have been written about effectively planning and marketing seminars, and we don't have enough space to go into a great deal of detail here. But there are some essential things to keep in mind if you decide to pursue this option:

Offering value. Figure out what you want attendees to take away from your seminar, both in terms of knowledge and skills and in terms of tangible items, like workbooks or other materials.

Selecting a location. Hotel meeting rooms are common locales for seminars, but you might get a better deal by using facilities at your local library, school, church, or municipal building.

Selecting a date. Saturdays are popular days for workshops and seminars, because more working people are able to attend. However, weekends often are packed with family activities and obligations, so evenings might be better for short seminars.

Setting a price. Research has shown that people who pay to attend seminars are more likely to show up on the day and more interested in the material presented. Set a price that fairly compensates you for your time and expertise but still provides value for the audience.

Marketing your seminar. There are many ways to publicize your seminar; do some research to find out which methods would be most effective in reaching your target audience. Remember that your response rate may be as low as one per 1,000, so plan your marketing budget wisely.

Also consider finding partners. If you're using your local library, for instance, maybe you can publicize your seminar in the library's newsletter to members. Maybe the chamber of commerce will waive its usual room rental fee in exchange for a set number of free tickets to give to its members. One of the beauties of do-it-yourself seminars is that you can be as creative as you like in pursuing opportunities, and, at the same time, adding a plank to your platform.

Making the Most of It

Whether you plug into conferences sponsored by someone else or design and promote your own, use these opportunities to sell your work as well as yourself. If you've had a book published, get permission from the conference sponsor to sell your book at the back of the meeting room. If you aren't getting paid (or if you aren't being paid very much), you should be able to negotiate a deal where you keep the profits—the difference between the wholesale and retail price—on books sold at the conference. If your fee for speaking or presenting is fairly high, the sponsor may want to keep the profits from book sales. That's not necessarily a bad deal; people who buy the book at the conference are desirable readers, and they are likely to pass on information about the conference, and your work, to their friends and colleagues.

Helpful Hints

At any public appearance, your attitude will either reinforce or destroy your image. Smile at your audience and the people who are purchasing your book; offer a quick hello; make eye contact. Even if you're tired and feeling cranky, pretend you're having a good time. You can drop the act when you're out of the public eye.

You can arrange to sign your books at conferences, but you shouldn't be the one to collect the money for back-of-room sales or announce that the books are available for purchase. Attendees generally don't like to feel that they've been set up for a sales pitch, and you'll come across as more of a shill than a respected authority figure if you're collecting money for your own book. If the conference organizer can't provide someone else to handle the actual transactions, recruit a friend or relative to do it for you.

Another way to handle the book issue is to include it in the cost of attending the conference or seminar. This can add perceived value for potential attendees, and it's nice to be able to say that 100 percent of the people who attend your events go away with a copy of your book in their hands. You can do something similar even if you don't have a book published yet; make good-quality copies of articles that you've written or that have quoted you on the topic of your presentation, and distribute these as hand-outs to attendees. This helps reinforce your profile in the minds of potential readers, who might become avid readers of future articles by and about you and maybe even eager purchasers of the book you're shopping to publishers.

Stay in Touch

People who have attended one of your presentations might be interested in others, which helps raise your profile and build your platform. Invite attendees to sign up for a newsletter (e-mail or snail mail) to keep them posted about upcoming events. Then use this mailing list to stay in touch with people who are already interested in you and your topic. A regular newsletter offering free and useful information has value for the recipient, and you can use it to help market your next conference or seminar, as well as your writing.

Web Sites and Blogs

The Internet offers a plethora of opportunities to raise your profile, if you know how to use it. Personal Web sites usually aren't the most effective way to reach large potential readerships; there are so many of them that it's real work to make yours stand out so surfers can find you. However, there are other Internet routes that can provide important support as you build your platform.

The Right Kind of Site

Design your Web site around what you want to write. That doesn't mean you should use your site to post your unpublished works; for one thing, posting on the Internet counts as publication, and potential publishers will be indifferent at best when you ask them to pay you for something that already has been made available to the world. Use your Web site to connect what you want to write with people who will want to read what you write. If your goal is to write fantasy stories, for instance, you might design a Web site for fans of established fantasy authors. If you can pack your site with fun and interesting information, you have a good chance of developing a strong following. Then, when you sell your first fantasy short story or novel, you can use the Web site to alert your visitors; you have a built-in conduit to help promote your own work.

Adding the Opt-In

With so many Web sites, many users are relying on RSS feeds to keep them updated on the topics and sites they care about. RSS is an acronym for Rich Site Summary, also known as Really Simple Syndication. It includes an opt-in feature, where site visitors sign up to have updates sent directly to their e-mail inboxes. RSS also makes it easy to share your site content with other sites, and your content gets listed in directories of RSS feeds—all of which can help expand the reach of your site.

Blogs

Short for Web log, a blog is an online journal. It can be on a single topic, like Our Daily Bread, or on broader subjects, like International News. It can have a single author or several regular contributors. It can be limited to the author's or contributors' postings, or it can be an interactive forum where readers can post replies and comments of their own. The key ingredient for any blog is fresh content. Most of the successful and popular blogs are updated every day, and many of them are updated several times a day. Blog readers get impatient when content isn't updated regularly, and, for them, a promising blog can go stale in just a day or two. That's one of the main drawbacks to blogging, especially for people who are juggling work and home life and trying to launch a writing career at the same time.

On the other hand, the most popular blogs boast devoted followings, and that makes this another tool you can use to build your platform. Especially in book publishing, agents and editors like to see evidence of a strong potential readership and effective ways to reach that readership. A popular blog related to your book topic gives you a unique avenue for marketing your work to interested readers.

Podcasting

Podcasting—the ability to broadcast audio from the Web—is still in its infancy, but, if it attains the same popularity as other Web-based functions, it could become a valuable new tool for promoting yourself and your work. Imagine hosting your own weekly radio show on the Internet, with the potential of reaching listeners around the world instantly and cheaply. You still have to figure out how to make sure your virtual audience can find you; like other Web-based opportunities, there's a lot of clutter to cut through. But, if podcasting takes off the way fan sites, blogs, and other Internet functions have, it might become another de rigueur element for writers to add to their marketing strategies.

You Can Become an Expert

If you select a specialty for your writing, you can at the same time build a name for yourself as an expert. The more published credits you have in, say, home-based businesses, the more attractive you are to the media, conference organizers, and even the legal professions as a knowledgeable source on the topic. The more recognition you get for your expertise, the easier it will be to sell your articles on the topic, and the more published clips you have, the easier it will be for you to branch out into other areas of writing.

There are all kinds of opportunities to develop and exploit such expertise, many of them discussed here and throughout this book. Choose your subject well; if you decide to take advantage of these opportunities, you'll be spending a lot of time writing, reading, and talking about it. Make sure your topic isn't one you'll get bored with quickly. If you're worried about that, pick a couple of topics, and split your time between them.

Build relationships with the media. Keep a separate Rolodex of any media contacts you make and keep in touch with those reporters and editors occasionally by providing them with new material. If you don't have new material of your own to provide, make suggestions for stories that aren't related to your projects. Being generous with ideas that don't directly benefit you helps build trust between you and a reporter or editor, and that trust pays off when you do have something of your own you want to cover.

Investing in professional relationships with the media, conference organizers, and others also gives you opportunities to borrow another's platform. An article about your latest speech in the local newspaper is more effective in building awareness than an ad covering the same material. Having your book available at a seminar sponsored by a professional association adds more credibility to your book than hawking it from your own Web site. A recommendation on a popular fiction blog to check out the short story you just had published is more compelling to readers than an announcement you send out yourself via e-mail. Being able to use other platforms like this isn't just efficient; it's an essential part of elevating your own platform.

Most beginning writers don't have many ways to set themselves apart from the passel of other writers anxious to get published. As hard as it is to break into the industry, you owe it to yourself to explore every possible avenue for convincing agents and editors to take a chance on you. Start building your platform at the beginning of your career, and it will serve you well even after you've established yourself as a professional writer.

Chapter 3

Find Your Place in this Writing World

A Matching Game: Ideas and Audience

New writers often make the mistake of thinking everyone will want to read their work. Pros know that a claim of universal appeal really is an admission that the writer doesn't know who her audience is. Without a clear idea of your readership, you're unlikely to find a buyer for your work, no matter how well-written it is.

How People Read

To start gaining insight into your potential readers, try thinking about how people read a daily newspaper. Nearly all major newspapers are divided into several sections—there may be one for local news, one for national and world news, one for sports, one for business, and one for lifestyle or recreation. No matter how big the newspaper's circulation is, it is highly unlikely that every subscriber reads every page of the newspaper every day. The reason newspapers separate the different categories of information is so their readers can more easily find the articles they actually want to read.

Helpful Hints

Fiction writers also benefit from imagining a single reader as a representative of their audience. As you write, pretend you're telling your story to one person; think of what questions the listener might ask, and when those questions should be answered to maximize suspense without causing confusion. This can help you handle pacing and plot points.

Magazine and book publishers work on the same principle. This is why magazines often are divided into "departments" or other sections and why book publishers—especially the major conglomerates—create imprint lines with narrower audiences. Consider Penguin Putnam, for example. This huge publishing house has twenty-one imprints in the United States, each focusing on specific types of books. The Sentinel imprint, one of its newest lines, publishes exclusively conservative titles such as Ronald Kessler's *A Matter of Character: Inside the White House of George W. Bush*. A book by a liberal author, or with a liberal slant, has no chance of being accepted at Sentinel, because Sentinel's readership is not liberal.

Even bestselling books don't appeal to everybody; they just appeal to an awful lot of people. You shouldn't try to appeal to everybody, either; if Michael Crichton and Agatha Christie can't do it, there's no reason to waste your energy trying. Instead, get in the habit of imagining a single reader who represents a composite of your audience. What are his interests? What kind of job does he have? What's his family life like? What does he like to do on a Saturday night? Most important, what does he already know about your topic, and what can you tell him about it that will be new, interesting, and useful?

Who Needs Your Project?

Writers are continually admonished to "write for the market." But what is the market? Instead of thinking about which newspapers, magazines, and book publishers might be interested in your work, look past those markets to the readers they serve. That's the real market you should be aiming for, because those readers will be the end users of your product. When you come up with a project that serves the needs of a specific section of the reading public, selling your work becomes much easier; all you have to do is find the publication that targets those same readers.

Consider this book as an example of this approach. The readers of the *Only Writing Series You'll Ever Need* generally are novices in the topics covered by the series. They need a grounding in the basics, plus enough detail to be thoroughly familiar with the topic, and resources for adding to their store of knowledge. *Only Writing Series You'll Ever Need* books are not meant to appeal to experts, so they're short on jargon and long on translating technical things into plain English. The information in *Only Writing Series You'll Ever Need* books is meant to be useful, practical, educational, and entertaining.

For many writers, especially those who are doing freelance assignments for publications, the readers you want to reach will change with each piece you do. Your tone, structure, angle, and vocabulary will differ depending on whether you're writing a story about Java script for a computer trade journal or one about effective Web page design for home-based businesses.

Get to Know Your Potential Markets

Agents and editors are always urging writers to study the markets they want to write for. One of the most irritating aspects of their jobs is the inordinate amount of time they spend opening queries and proposals that aren't right for them. With all the information available to you from a plethora of sources, there is no reason not to do your research before you begin marketing your work. Besides, the better you know the market, the fewer rejections you're apt to get—simply because you won't be sending inappropriate material.

Directory Listings

Market directories like *Writer's Market* provide essential information about what various publications and book publishers are looking for. Just as important, these listings also often include things the market is not interested in. *Antique and Collectables Newsmagazine*'s listing, for example, clearly states that it is not interested in opinion pieces, religious articles, or exposés. *Listen Magazine*'s listing notes that it has been flooded with pitches about drunk driving and recommends that hopeful writers consider different topics. *Family*

Circle magazine's listing shows that it is not interested in fiction or poetry.

All these listings are clear and direct, in black and white. Yet, the editors at these magazines still spend hours each week responding to pitches for exactly the wrong kind of writing. Editors get frustrated because they have to spend time on these submissions, which they can ill afford and which they would much rather spend reading submissions that are right for them. Writers get frustrated because they collect a whole bunch of rejections, most likely form letters, and never really understand why no one likes their ideas.

Helpful Hints

Many professional writers advise making a list of five to ten potential markets for your idea, then prioritizing those markets based on your research. The markets that are looking for your topic or slant on an article go at the top of your list. Read the listings and match the market's needs with your idea.

To be fair, it's also frustrating when you come up with a great idea for a story and think you've got a perfectly matching market, and then find, when you read the listing for that market, that it isn't interested in the type of idea you just came up with. Unfortunately, that goes with the territory. The only thing you can do is keep reading through the market listings, looking for one that is a good fit with your idea and is open to it.

Read the Publication

There is no substitute for reading the publication you hope to break into. You don't have to be a subscriber, but you should be able to identify—and replicate—the style and tone of various articles. Pay attention to how features are structured. Do they emphasize expert sources, or are they more "real people" oriented? Do they contain a lot of pithy quotes, or are the articles more narrative in nature? Does every feature have a sidebar?

Look at smaller pieces, too. These often are excellent break-in points for new writers, and a series of small pieces can lead to bigger assignments. Departments sometimes have different editorial voices than the main articles, so pay attention to style and tone here, too.

How to Think Like an Editor

Editors have to think about stories that serve the needs of their readers. Writers who learn to think like editors—who get beyond the giddy imaginings of seeing their bylines in a major publication and focus on serving the readers—are more likely to come up with ideas that editors will appreciate. Remember that, as a writer, you are providing a service; readers, not editors, are your ultimate consumers.

Spotting Trends

Cashing in on trends is tricky because the publishing process takes so long. By the time you've done your research and sent off your query, the latest fad could already be on its way out. This is true for magazines and books, less so for newspapers, which publish daily or weekly and so can be more timely in their coverage. Still, magazine and book publishers do like trendy topics, as long as the trend still has "legs"—that is, it's likely to continue long enough to make running a story or printing a book worthwhile. When you're considering a trend topic, keep the actual publishing schedule in mind:

Researching and polishing your idea: one to two weeks for a magazine story; one to two months for a book proposal

Response time from a potential market: one to three months for most magazines; up to six months for agents and book publishers, depending on what material you send

Writing time: four to six weeks for a magazine article; six months or more for a book

Publication date: one to six months after you've turned your story in for a magazine; six to eighteen months for a book

Unfortunately, the realities of the publishing business make a lot of "trend" stories worthless to magazine and book publishers, and therefore not nearly as valuable to you. As noted, you might have better luck pitching such stories to newspapers, which have much quicker turnaround times.

Helpful Hints

The death of a trend sometimes can be a good story idea, too. Maybe the resurgence of natural farming is part of the demise of big corporate farms, which have been the trend for many years now. Connecting these two things in a sensible, accurate story could be the story idea that gets a resounding yes from an editor.

How can you tell if a trend has legs? It's part research and part good instincts. Be on the alert for similar stories that crop up in the news media. If you hear a story on NPR about organic gardening one day, then read an Associated Press article in your local newspaper a week later about hormone-free livestock, and a few days later see a television news magazine piece about so-called "green" pesticides and herbicides, you might be looking at a growing trend toward more natural agricultural practices. You'll probably have to act quickly to get a salable story idea out of this, because, unfortunately, you aren't the only one looking for trends, and no publisher wants to be second in covering a hot topic.

Adding Value

Whenever you come up with an idea, think of ways to make it most interesting and useful to the reader. Editors tend to think in terms of packages, or how the proposed idea will look once it's printed. Adding the appropriate package elements to your pitch can help an editor visualize how your idea fits in with her needs.

For magazine articles, think in terms of sidebars and graphic elements. Sidebars are short pieces that are related to the main story; common sidebar themes are checklists, mini bios or profiles of people quoted in the main piece, and little-known facts about the main topic. Study publications to see how they use sidebars and their average length. Graphic elements include photos, illustrations, and charts.

Helpful Hints

You do not have to provide your own photos and graphics. Many magazines purchase these from freelancers, but nearly all of them prefer to deal with professional photographers and graphic designers. Most writers just provide suggestions for photos, illustrations, and charts.

For book proposals, "adding value" might include these elements, too. But, often, agents and editors see more value in things like endorsements from celebrities or well-known experts on your book topic, or having one of these celebrities or experts write a foreword for your book. Another way of adding value to your pitch is to highlight your credentials and platform to show why you are the right person to write your book.

Finding and Filling Voids

Beginning writers often feel that all the really good ideas have been taken, and they doubt their own abilities to come up with anything fresh. After you've been seriously pursuing your writing for a while, though, you'll find that the real difficulty is having too many ideas clamoring for your attention. It takes some practice to learn which ideas have real potential and which need to simmer a little longer, but that ability comes to most writers eventually.

Starting the Search

The basics are still the most reliable ways to generate ideas for articles, short stories, novels, and nonfiction books. Examine what you know, what you've experienced, what you like, and what you'd like to learn more about. Make a list of these things, and then make a list of questions about each item. Those questions can lead to great ideas, if only because they prompt you to think about familiar topics in new ways.

Say you like cheesecake. Do you know anything about its history? Who invented it and when? How have the taste and texture changed over the years? When did it become a chic dessert, with all sorts of different flavors and sauces? Is there such a thing as a cheesecake hall of fame, or maybe a cheesecake tour, similar to wine tours? Did it fall out of favor during the low-carb craze? Is it making a comeback? Just a handful of questions can open the door to all kinds of possibilities.

Read as much as you can from as many different sources as you can. News stories can spark great ideas for fiction and nonfiction, especially if you get into the habit of asking yourself "what if" questions when you read. What if the self-replicating robots you read about just kept replicating themselves forever, not out of any weird mechanical consciousness but just because that's what they're programmed to do? What if Pope Benedict XVI had been from South America instead of Europe? What if the identity of Watergate's Deep Throat had been revealed while Richard Nixon was still alive? Again, just asking questions can generate more ideas than you could possibly write about.

Looking for Holes

The key to finding—and therefore being able to fill—a void is figuring out what has been overlooked by others. Look for perspectives that haven't been explored. If you want to write about getting organized, find out whether anything has been done on the effectiveness of services that come to your home and clean out your closets. Do those closets stay organized after a month, three months, a year? Or do they provide only a temporary respite to the chronically disorganized? Has anyone covered the cheerfully disorganized, or how to forgive yourself for being disorganized? How about the psychological aspects of being organized versus being disorganized?

Helpful Hints

Keep an eye out for stories that don't reflect your experience or opinion. If you don't fit the mold assumed by a particular article or book, it's a good bet that other people don't fit it, either. It's also a good bet that you've just stumbled across an ignored perspective.

The same can be done for nearly any topic. There are forests of articles and books on career planning, for example; are there any aimed at people who enjoy the jobs they have and don't necessarily want to move up the corporate ladder? Is there any advice out there for people who supervise these employees about how to keep them motivated and engaged? Maybe this is a hole waiting to be filled.

Check Out the Competition

The Internet has made it easier than ever to find out what else has been written on your topic. Sites like Findarticles.com continually troll the Web and archive articles from a multitude of publications. You can search articles by keyword and publications by topic, and many of the articles are free.

Use online booksellers like Amazon.com and BarnesandNoble.com to get information about in-print and upcoming books. You can find out the publisher, the format, and often the table of contents or excerpts of competing books—information that will help you identify both potential publishers and the weak spots in the competition.

Findarticles.com also provides a portal to a broad spectrum of useful statistical information sites, such as the Statistics of Income bulletin from the IRS and the Uniform Crime Bulletin from the FBI. If you're not sure where to look for information and a Google search doesn't turn up what you want, sites like this provide useful alternative searches.

Establishing an Angle

As we've shown, the mere fact that somebody else has beaten you to your topic doesn't mean you don't have a good idea. All it means is that you have to do a little more work to establish your angle. The techniques described here will help you develop the habit of thinking beyond what already has been done. You might even be surprised at how quickly you become adept at finding new approaches to not-so-new ideas.

Finding the Right Market

You've made your list of topics, asked your questions, researched what other people have written, and identified a good angle for your idea. Now you have to match that angle with potential markets, and that goes back to reading the directory listings and studying the publications. (This is why we started out with the chicken-or-the-egg question. Experienced writers travel this same circle many times over, and they usually get to the point where it doesn't really matter where they start, because they'll cover all of the same ground in any case.)

Helpful Hints

Market directories often include profiles of publishers' readers, especially for magazines. This should be a standard part of your research activity, even if you're planning to write a book. Magazines that target the same readers you want to reach with your book can help you demonstrate a market for your book and help you further refine your angle.

Remember, too, that your ultimate responsibility, whatever you're writing, is to serve your readers. That means honing your angle to make it a near-perfect match with the market. So, if your story is about the employee who is content to do her job, does it well, and isn't interested in a promotion, and your target readers are human resource managers, your angle might have to incorporate a discussion of the value of keeping these employees as well as creative incentives to retain them.

What about Fiction?

Much of the information we've presented here applies largely to nonfiction. But fiction writers also have many of the same considerations, and many of the techniques for generating nonfiction ideas can be just as effective in creating plots and characters for fiction. Also, fiction writers have the same need to understand and meet the needs of their readers. Fans of specific genres expect certain things from their authors, for instance, and that means the editors who purchase fiction will look for those things, too. Writers of children's stories have to be especially aware of vocabulary and tone to ensure they are appropriate for the targeted age group.

In marketing your fiction, it also is helpful to know what has been done before. Book editors want to know where a novel will fit on a bookstore shelf, so it's useful if you can compare your story or style with a well-known author's. If you say that your mystery is reminiscent of Dorothy Sayers or Ellery Queen, a prospective agent or editor will know just what style of mystery you've written.

Helpful Hints

Be careful of your phrasing when you compare your work with another author's. If you call yourself the next John LeCarré or Ernest Hemingway, you'll probably turn off the agent or editor you're trying to impress. Say instead that your style is like Hemingway's, or that your story is similar to a LeCarré novel.

Finding out what others have done in fiction also is a good way to research potential markets. Check out published books in your genre at your local bookstore or library and make note of which publishers are putting out your kind of novel. Check the acknowledgments in these books, too. Authors who single out their agents or editors in the acknowledgments have had a good experience working with these people, and these could be good leads for you. As always, double-check any information you glean here with the various directories to find out how to approach these agents and publishers.

Keeping an Open Mind

Nearly every writer has run into this problem at one time or another: You've got way more information than you can use for your article, and you're having a hard time deciding what to leave out. As agonizing as it can be to make the hard cuts, this actually could be turned into a bonus for you.

Helpful Hints

New writers sometimes think that shorter pieces are easier to write than longer ones. Actually, the reverse is true. It can be difficult to squeeze all the pertinent information you need into 1,200 words. It's even harder to do it in 800 words. You have to be very good at your craft to crack the small openings in major publications.

One possible solution to this problem is to turn your article idea into a package by using the excess information for sidebars. Another possibility is to divide your information into two or more standalone story ideas; one could be for a general audience, for example, and another for readers who are more expert on the topic, perhaps a trade journal. With the proper research and refining, you could get two or more articles for two or more non-competing markets—in effect doubling the return on your investment of time and energy.

The great thing about researching markets and ideas is that there is always a new angle waiting to be discovered, and it isn't as hard as it may seem. If you keep an open mind in considering ideas and markets, you'll soon find that you, like the seasoned professionals, are able to separate good ideas from bad ones and decide which ones deserve a closer examination.

Chapter 4

Working with an Agent

"Do I Need an Agent?"

Whether you need an agent depends in large part on where you are in your writing career and what you're trying to sell. If your focus is selling features or short stories to magazines, you don't need an agent, and, in fact, you wouldn't be able to find a reputable agent to represent this kind of work because the commissions would be too small. You also usually don't need an agent to represent your children's books, and you may not need one for your adult fiction or nonfiction books, depending on which publishers you hope to interest.

Helpful Hints

Advances and royalties tend to be low for children's books, which is why most agents don't handle them; it isn't worth their time when they can't expect much of a commission. Publishers of children's books understand this and are happy to deal directly with authors.

For the Big Players

If your aim is to land a contract with one of the major publishing houses, you probably will need an agent to represent your work. About 80 percent of the books these conglomerates publish are purchased through agents. Some of the largest houses won't even consider submissions from unagented writers; when they get manuscripts directly from the author, the author usually gets a short note in reply advising him to get an agent.

The advantage to the big publishers in dealing only with agents is that agents know what editors are looking for and won't submit work that isn't salable. The agent's reputation, and therefore his ability to succeed as an agent, rides on submitting only the best—not just in terms of ideas, but also in terms of presentation and research—to only those editors who are appropriate for the project. The publisher saves enormous time and expense by allowing agents to do the work of sifting through submissions to find the real gems.

The advantage to you as a writer is that the agent has the contacts, experience, and information to market your book idea to the proper people. Good agents stay informed of which editor is in charge of which topics or lines at which publishing house, and they often get tips from editors about what kind of material they're looking for. When you have an agent, you're putting his expertise to work for you.

Mid-Sized Publishers

Smaller publishers don't have the clout of the major houses, and they don't usually have the resources to offer enormous advances or extensive marketing campaigns. On the other hand, these houses tend to be more open to new authors than the big multinational firms. Although these publishers, like any business, always are on the lookout for commercial successes, they also tend to be more interested than the big houses in titles that won't necessarily capture a huge readership or debut at number one on the bestseller lists, such as literary fiction or niche nonfiction.

Helpful Hints

Publishing directories such as *Writer's Market* usually indicate whether a publisher accepts submissions directly from writers or whether they accept only agented submissions. If you're undecided about whether to get an agent, first look up the publishers you're most interested in and see what their requirements are.

Many of the mid-sized publishers will work with unagented writers, but, like the big houses, they prefer to work with agents.

The reasons are the same: Agents know what editors are looking for, weed out the unworkable, and are familiar with the ins and outs of publishing. An agent also should be able to negotiate a better advance and more favorable terms with the mid-sized publisher than you could on your own.

Small Presses

Many small presses will work directly with authors, and some even prefer not to deal with agents. Likewise, many agents prefer not to deal with small presses because they generally are unable to offer the average advances of their mid-sized competitors. A good agent will seek out the best advance for her authors, and the small presses know they can't compete with bigger houses. By the same token, agents often relegate the small houses to the bottom of their contact lists, going to them only if and when larger houses pass on a project.

The same goes for university presses. They typically offer minimal advances, and sometimes none at all, which makes them unattractive to agents. As a result, they are open to unagented writers, and many university presses have expanded their catalogs to include titles with a broader, mass-market appeal rather than strictly academic ones.

The Job of an Agent

In its simplest form, an agent's job consists of matching supply and demand, with writers supplying the goods and publishers determining whether there's a demand for the goods. A good agent keeps up on industry news and keeps up her contacts; when she has a good relationship with an editor at one publisher, she'll keep that relationship on a solid footing when the editor moves to another publisher, even if the new publisher is one the agent hasn't dealt with before.

An agent usually has a two- or three-stage marketing plan for the projects she represents. Her goal is to find a publisher that will be both enthusiastic about and appropriate for the project and one that will offer the best terms for the author. If the first choices on her list pass, she'll move on to the second-tier choices.

A typical agent's day will be spent largely on the phone and the computer, dealing with editors and clients. In a single phone call or e-mail exchange with an editor, he may negotiate a contract, pitch new projects the editor might be interested in, and discuss problems with a writer's text or deadline. In talking with a client, he might discuss feedback he has received on the author's latest proposal, help the author overcome some difficulty on a manuscript, and talk about publicity opportunities. The agent is a master juggler, continually shifting gears to make sure the highest priorities get taken care of first while keeping the rest of his to-do list from falling through the cracks. The unexpected can always change an agent's daily plan, but her main priorities usually fall in the following order:

1. **New contracts.** After the negotiating is finished, the publisher sends a contract to the agent. The agent reviews this to make sure everything covered in the negotiations is reflected in the written document, then forwards it to the author for his or her signature. This is almost always the agent's first priority, barring some unforeseen glitch.

2. **Publishers' payments.** When the contract is signed by the author and publisher, the publisher returns a copy of it (called the "executed contract" when all parties have signed) and the first advance payment to the agent. The agent deposits the publisher's check and writes a new one to the author, minus the agent's commission.

3. **Negotiating contracts.** After taking care of finalized deals and payments, the agent concentrates on negotiating the details on pending contract offers. Each contract is different because each publisher and each author have their own needs; the publisher may want a "next-book" clause, while the author may have to be free to do a collaboration with someone else for a different

publisher. It can take a lot of time to get the details just right for every contract.

4. **Marketing other projects.** After she handles all the contracts, payments, and pending offers, the agent can focus on pitching projects to editors. She may do this in the same phone call to the editor she's negotiating a contract with, if that editor would be appropriate for the new project, or she may write separate query letters or e-mails to editors on her marketing list.

Only after all these priorities have been taken care of (and assuming no emergencies arise) will an agent start reading through the piles of new submissions from prospective clients. Very often, an agent doesn't have time to do this until the end of the business day; sometimes he will put new submissions aside until the weekend so he can get more pressing business done during the week. This is why it takes so long for agents to respond to queries and proposals. They simply don't have time to get to them any sooner.

What to Look for

You want an agent because she has expertise and contacts in the publishing industry. You also want one who is reputable and honest in her business dealings, and who has a good track record of sales to royalty-paying publishers. Finally, you want an agent who is reasonably enthusiastic about you and your project.

Specialization

Few, if any, agents handle every type of book on the market these days. The publishing business is highly competitive and changes rapidly, making it virtually impossible for any single agent to keep up with trends and currents in every single book category. Like the publishing houses they sell to, agents tend to specialize, sometimes in specific genres like romance and women's fiction, or in broader categories like adult nonfiction.

This tendency toward specialization is good for you as a writer. First, it makes it easier for you to find an agent who is familiar with the market and publishing climate for your type of book and who has contacts with publishers who could be interested in your project. Second, an agent who has placed several similar books with publishers likely is respected by the editors he deals with, and that respect will rub off on the editor's perception of you and your work when the agent submits it.

Fair Dealing

Reputable agents make their money by selling clients' books to publishers. They do not charge up-front fees for anything—not for reading your submission, offering critiques, marketing your work, drawing up the author-agent agreement, or anything else. If an agent asks you to pay for anything before offering to represent you, the odds are good that you're being scammed.

The Association of Author's Representatives (AAR) sets codes of conduct for literary agents. This code prohibits up-front fees and requires agents to have separate business and personal accounts so that clients' funds don't get mixed in with the agent's personal money. The AAR also prohibits members from participating in any sort of kickback scheme, such as referring potential clients to an editing service or a self-publisher in which the agent has a financial interest.

Not all reputable agents are members of the AAR, for a variety of reasons. Some may not have met the sales requirements to join (the AAR requires new members to have sold ten titles in the past eighteen months), while others may feel that the expense of joining outweighs the benefits of being a member. However, reputable agents who are not members generally follow the AAR's ethical standards.

Track Record

The ultimate test of a successful agent is sales to royalty-paying publishers. Sometimes you'll find a list of recent titles an agent has sold in the major directories, but most agents won't discuss specific sales with anyone except the client and the publisher to whom the book was sold. When you're seeking representation, you'll have to be satisfied with more general information. An agent should be willing to tell you how many titles he has sold in the past year or whether one of the books he represented was a bestseller, for example, but he should not discuss details of any sales, such as the advance the author received.

Helpful Hints

New agents aren't necessarily new to the publishing industry. Sometimes editors will leave the publisher side of the business and set themselves up as agents, and they usually have enough knowledge of the business and enough contacts to make good agents. Other new agents might have worked as assistants to established agents for several years before striking out on their own.

According to the AAR, new agents—who, often, are most open to representing first-time authors—should begin making sales in six to twelve months. An agent who has been in business two years and has yet to sell a manuscript may not be either inept or unconnected, but these circumstances don't bode well for your project. Look for an agent who has a strong record of sales for titles that are similar to yours.

Enthusiasm

When you get a positive response from an agent, it means she thinks your work has a reasonable chance of getting a publisher's attention. Very likely, she'll have some ideas for improving your manuscript or proposal to make it more attractive and salable. She may even suggest a new slant that will really make it stand out. But a good agent won't go overboard with visions of success. Publishing is a volatile and vicarious business, and this month's hot book market could be equally as cold next month. No one, not even the most experienced agent, can predict the next bestseller or the story that will earn millions in movie rights. Be wary of agents who promise you the moon; it probably means they don't have their feet on the ground.

By the same token, an agent who reminds you of Eeyore in the Winnie the Pooh stories probably isn't going to be the most effective representative for you, either. Pessimism, like optimism, is infectious. An agent who sounds glum when he's pitching your project to an editor is unlikely to score a request for the proposal, much less a sale.

Finding the Right Agent for You

You've got a list of reputable, experienced agents, ones who are well-respected, open to new clients, and with whom you think you would feel comfortable doing business. But, as important as those qualities are, they don't necessarily mean these agents are right for you or your work. A big part of finding the right agent is matching your material to an agent's specialty. An agent who focuses on fiction is likely to be of little help in marketing your how-to book for beginning cabinet-makers, even if you could capture her interest.

Some literary agencies will accept new writers only if they are referred by existing clients, and it's a waste of your time and energy to try to "sneak" into these agencies. Instead, concentrate your energies on the many agents who are ever on the lookout for talented writers with promising book ideas.

Directories

There are several reliable directories that list agents and what they're looking for. Writer's Digest *Guide to Literary Agents* is readily available at major bookstores and is updated regularly. You also can check out the AAR's online directory of agents at *www.writers.net/agents.html*.

Another excellent resource is *Literary Marketplace*, known as the LMP. Although the price of the LMP makes it an impractical purchase for most beginning writers, good-sized public libraries usually have the latest print edition in their reference sections. LMP now has an online database, and you can get access to parts of it for free, although you do have to register. LMP also recently introduced a one-week paid subscription, which gives you access to all of the LMP features online for about $20. This can be cost-effective if you consolidate searches for agents and publishers, both of which are available through LMP, or if you plan to do your research at times when your public library is closed.

Helpful Hints

Print directories usually list agents' telephone numbers and may even include fax numbers and e-mail addresses. This is not an invitation for you to call the agent to pitch your project, or to fax your entire proposal or manuscript to him. Read and follow the submission guidelines in the listing.

The value of these directories is that they spell out such things as how the agent prefers to be contacted—regular mail, e-mail, etc.—as well as what they accept from prospective clients. Some ask for queries only and will return, unopened, unsolicited proposals and manuscripts. Others specify a synopsis and the first three chapters for novels, or an overview and a sample chapter for nonfiction. Very often, these directories also will list what a particular agent will not consider or does not want; some will accept simultaneous submissions, for example, and some won't.

On the Bookshelf

Another way to match an agent with your material is to visit your local bookseller and check out the acknowledgments pages in books that are similar to yours. You can reasonably assume that authors who include their agents in the acknowledgments have a good relationship with their agent and are pleased with their agent's representation. The fact that the author has written a book similar to yours shows that the agent handles your kind of material. If you use this method to gather potential agents' names, you can then check out their listings in the print directories to find out how best to approach them.

Author-Agent Agreements

Agents make money by convincing publishers to buy their clients' books. To be effective, an agent has to have the exclusive right to market your book. Otherwise, any given editor could be getting pitched for the same project from multiple sources, and you can imagine the chaos that would result. Some agents forego formal agreements until your work is sold, but this can be risky for both of you. Without a written contract, the agent has no way of knowing whether he's the only one marketing your book; if you decide to look for another agent, you have no way of knowing that the first agent isn't still pitching your project; and, if a dispute arises over the agent's commission or expenses, you have no written document to resolve the issue.

A written agreement, spelling out the terms and obligations for each of you, really is the best way to protect your interests and the agent's. It should be signed before the agent does anything in the way of presenting your work to his contacts, and each of you should have a signed copy for your files.

Scope of Representation

The meat of the author-agent agreement is the scope of representation. Often, you give the agent the exclusive right to represent all of your book-length work, regardless of the format and no matter where potential publishers might be located. Agents who offer these kinds of agreements are looking to build a relationship with new writers, with the expectation that the partnership will be lucrative for both of you over the long term. Indeed, agents (and publishers) often don't expect to make a lot of money right away with new writers;

substantial profits are more likely to come from second, third, fourth or even fifth books. An author-agent agreement that covers all your work, then, can be taken as an expression of faith in your future success.

Note that the agent is only interested in book-length work. It is exceedingly rare for agents to handle short stories, magazine articles, or poetry. For one thing, you don't need an agent to submit these pieces to appropriate publishers. For another, the agent's commission on these pieces would be far too small to justify spending his time marketing them.

Helpful Hints

Many agents offer short-term, one-book contracts with new authors. This gives both of you a chance to see how you work together without locking you into a long-term relationship. If things go well and you decide you want to continue the partnership, you can consider a more comprehensive agreement.

In some circumstances, you might want to give an agent exclusive rights to only one specific project. It might be appropriate if, for example, you have one agent for your nonfiction books and need someone with expertise in marketing your adventure novel. In that case, your agreements with each agent must include explicit definitions of what the agent is entitled to represent.

Duration of the Contract

Most author-agent agreements are valid for one to two years, although some offer six-month contracts. Initial contracts usually cannot be terminated for a set period—six to twelve months on a one- or two-year contract, for example. This gives the agent time to market your work without fear that her right to represent you will be arbitrarily pulled. Some agents may require you to sign a new contract when the old one expires, but often there is simply a clause in the contract that allows for automatic renewal. Likewise, there usually is a provision that allows either party to terminate the contract—after the initial no-termination period—with one to three months' written notice to the other.

Agent's Commission

Any agency contract must spell out the agent's commission on sales. The industry standard is 15 percent for domestic sales and 20 to 25 percent for foreign sales. There may be higher commissions specified for things like movie rights, too. These higher commissions are warranted because such sales usually involve hiring a subagent—one based in the foreign country where your book is being marketed, or one who specializes in movie options and rights—and your agent's commission will have to be split with the subagent.

How Payments Are Handled

The author-agent agreement also describes how payments from publishers are handled. The agent will be authorized to accept all payments from publishers, including advances and royalty payments, on your behalf, which means that the publisher's check will be made out to the agent, not to you. The agent then writes you a check for those payments, minus the agent's commission. The agreement also may specify that the agent must forward payment to you within so many days after the check from the publisher clears the agent's bank.

Other Provisions

Most agreements include a "warranties and representations" clause, in which you promise that the work your agent is representing is your own. This is virtually the same clause you'll find in most publisher contracts and is designed to protect the agent against representing plagiarized works. There also may be a "hold-harmless" provision, in which the agent is protected from any liability if your work is plagiarized or otherwise violates someone's civil, privacy, or intellectual property rights.

Agreements also usually include a guarantee that you own the work. That is, you are promising the agent that you haven't sold any rights in the work anywhere else or turned over future earnings to someone else. If you have sold some rights (e.g., your novel is based on the same plot as a short story you had published, or a chapter of your book originally appeared as a feature article in a magazine) or turned over future earnings (to satisfy a debt or as part of a divorce decree, for instance), be sure to inform the agent of this before you sign any representation agreement. Full disclosure at the beginning of your relationship will avert lots of potential problems later on.

Helpful Hints

Some Internet writing sites encourage writers to post completed works or works in progress for review and comments from other writers. You may get valuable feedback this way, but remember that placing your work on the Internet counts as publication, and you'll have to disclose this to agents and editors who might be interested.

Sustaining a Professional Relationship

Some writers expect agents to be a combination of writing coach, cheerleader, psychologist, and best friend. In fact, sometimes an agent is all those things for her clients. But the author-agent relationship is essentially a business partnership. An agent's job is to sell her clients' work to publishers. Your job is to write material that publishers will be interested in. You and your agent may like each other personally. You might even end up being friends. But, if that friendship arises, it will grow from a sound professional relationship, based on realistic expectations of what your agent can, should, and will do for you.

Decide whether you want an agent before you begin marketing your book. An agent is less likely to be interested in representing you if you approach him only after a dozen editors have turned you down, because it's going to be hard for that agent to sell a manuscript that has already been rejected by editors he might want to contact.

Respect the Agent's Time

Agents are busy people, and business hours are overflowing with a long list of tasks that need to get done as soon as possible. Unnecessary interruptions that eat into the agent's precious and limited time are annoying and can sabotage your relationship. Most questions can be handled through e-mail, which is less intrusive than a phone call and often more convenient for the agent, since e-mail can be sent anytime. If you absolutely have to talk to your agent, write her a quick e-mail asking for a phone date and telling her, succinctly, what you need to discuss. When you do call her, always ask if she has time to talk with you, and be understanding if the answer is no. She may be in the middle of negotiations or some other critical task, and the hard truth is that, sometimes, you are not her highest priority.

Respect the Agent's Knowledge

One of the reasons you sought an agent is because you wanted to take advantage of his expertise in publishing. When he gives you advice on how to polish your proposal or work with your editor or pursue publicity opportunities, he is sharing his hard-earned knowledge of the business with you. That doesn't mean you have to do everything your agent recommends or be afraid to ask questions. But do recognize that your agent's goal is to help you succeed—success for you means success for him—and listen graciously to your agent's point of view.

Helpful Hints

If an agent gives you constructive feedback on your project before you've signed with her and you decide to make the suggested changes, be sure to give her first crack at your proposal after you've done so. She's obviously interested, and she has given you free advice on how to improve your work. In exchange, you should give her another chance to represent you.

If you're a first-time book author, your agent is not just an invaluable guide and ally in the publishing world; she's something of a visionary. She has taken on the responsibility of helping launch your career, with no guarantee that she will ever be compensated for her time, access, or expertise. Understanding and respecting your agent's contribution to your career is a critical component of a successful and professional relationship. After all, you are embarking on a business partnership, which, with the proper care, will reward both of you, monetarily and otherwise.

Chapter 5

Tackle the Magazine Market

How Magazine Publishing Works

The thing most writers need to understand about magazine publishing is the enormous lead times involved. Monthly magazines usually are working three to six months in advance; quarterlies may be working six to nine months ahead. Weeklies have shorter lead times, but they also usually have regular staff writers and generally don't provide as many opportunities for the newcomer or freelancer.

It's important to know this because any story ideas you have that are pegged to events or seasons have to be planned and submitted far ahead of time. If you want to do something about Father's Day or summer weekend getaways, for example, you probably will have to have your idea solidified and ready to send out in query form no later than February, while holiday craft or cooking ideas need to be in the editor's hands by midsummer.

Editorial Calendars

Many magazines try to help writers (and advertisers, who also are keenly interested in reaching the right audience at the right time) with their planning by issuing editorial calendars that spell out topics or themes for upcoming issues, as well as advertising and copy deadlines. Some magazines include query deadlines for specific issues. Calendars often are available on the magazine's Web site and may be included in the submission guidelines; they also may indicate special or extra editions, such as *Sports Illustrated*'s annual swimsuit issue.

Savvy writers make a practice of collecting and updating editorial calendars for their target publications. It's an easy way to remind yourself to think ahead, and it can act as a tickler when you're feeling stuck and idea-less. It's also helpful when you're trying to break into new markets, because it gives you important clues as to what the editors will be looking for and when.

Timing the Timeless

Timeless stories are ones that don't have a particular news peg to hang on. Many interview and profile pieces, for instance, can be published at any time. The disadvantage for you is that timeless articles are easy to push off the table of contents in favor of stories with more immediate appeal, thus delaying publication and the addition of another clip to your file. Another thing to consider: Editors generally prefer stories that have some sense of immediacy, because readers generally prefer them, too. You can earn marks for freshness by adding an element of timeliness to perennial stories. You might tie a story about sales of hybrid cars to the annual Earth Day observance, for example, or you might take the standby New Year's Resolution piece and adapt it for students in September as New School Year Resolutions.

It takes a little creativity and extra work to add timeliness to essentially timeless stories, but it can be done. Editors are more likely to snap up interviews or profiles when the subject is about to hit a milestone of some sort—releasing a new movie, say, or facing his third ballot for entry into the Baseball Hall of Fame. The added news value makes the story more compelling for editors and for readers.

Cultivate Patience

As long as the lead times are, most writers feel that the response times from magazines are even longer. It doesn't seem to make sense, at least to eager writers, that editors take weeks or months to respond to a simple query. In fact, because of the way most magazines handle submissions, it's a little surprising that it doesn't take longer.

Here's what happens when you send in your query—assuming that you've sent it to the right person. The editor in charge of screening submissions usually separates them into two piles. The first pile (and, by far, the largest) is the rejection pile for material that doesn't fit the magazine's needs. In most cases, rejections will get the fastest responses—assuming you've included your SASE.

Helpful Hints

For nonfiction articles, write a query that describes your idea and demonstrates that you know the subject and have access to experts. For fiction, magazine editors generally prefer to see a complete manuscript. Because of the volume of submissions they receive, editors often don't reply to fiction submissions unless they want to publish the story.

The second pile is for the "maybes," material the editor likes. But, at most magazines, this editor doesn't have the final decision on whether to purchase an article. Instead, she'll schedule a story conference with her boss (the managing editor, executive editor, or editor in chief); that conference also may include other editors and staff. Just arranging the conference can be a challenge because unanticipated crises, special projects, business travel, and vacations all have to be worked around. So, that conference might not even take place until several weeks after the editor has read your query.

Helpful Hints

What if your idea is on hold at a magazine? You can wait on the magazine to decide whether and when to assign or publish your material, or you can withdraw it and shop it to other markets. Always let the editor know what you intend to do; she'll be peeved if you offer it elsewhere without telling her.

When the conference does take place, your idea will be discussed, and one of three things will happen: The boss will reject it; the boss will accept it, and the editor will make a note to herself to call you to discuss payment, length, and so on; or the boss will say "maybe," in which case you should (but won't always) receive a note or e-mail from the editor letting you know that your idea is on hold.

Spotting Break-In Opportunities

Different types of magazines offer different openings for writers to exploit. The standard advice, and the usual path for beginning writers, is to look for short assignments, prove yourself to an editor with those, and then start pushing for bigger articles and more pay. It also helps if you can think like an editor—especially if you understand his needs and concerns.

Think Cover Blurb

Whatever your idea is, try to envision it on the cover of the magazine you're targeting. A bold headline and deck—the copy under the headline that gives a little more information about the story—are designed to catch the reader's eye and interest. Editors spend hours on the cover blurbs for each issue because strong blurbs can spur single-copy sales at the newsstand or supermarket checkout. If you can come up with a good head and deck for your idea, you've not only got the hook for your query, you've got a good chance of making an editor take notice.

Helpful Hints

A rule of thumb in magazine publishing is that, if you've seen a story in one publication, you're probably too late to cash in on a trend of similar stories. By the time another magazine could purchase and publish a similar article, the trend will be over.

Go Against the Flow

Controversy sells. Challenge conventional wisdom, and present facts and expert opinions to expose a nontraditional view. Many editors like these pieces because they get people talking. Readers respond to them because they expect to learn something new.

Offer Many Dimensions

A well-rounded article idea explores more than one facet of the story, and editors like to see depth in their major features. You can add dimensions and layers to almost any topic, often through the use of sidebars or other package elements (another thing editors like to see). A story on summer grilling might include a sidebar about unusual items to grill, like foie gras, for example, or one on the conflicting evidence about whether eating charcoal-grilled foods is good for you.

Get to Know the Publication

Virtually every magazine listing in every market directory implores writers to study the publication, but few give you any concrete advice on what to look for. Aside from seeing what topics a publication covers and what articles have been published recently, studying a publication means getting a feel for its style, tone, and editorial preferences. Analyzing the content can transport you into an editor's head, if you know what to look for. For every magazine you study, ask yourself these questions:

- **What categories do the feature articles fall into?** Are they mainly "how-to" or service articles? Does the magazine include a lot of profiles or interviews with celebrities or other people of interest? Is the focus on self-help, showing the reader how to accomplish a goal or task?
- **What is the editorial format?** Does each issue include a profile, an essay, a service article, and an investigative piece? Is each issue themed, so that all the articles are on a related topic? Or is the magazine divided into departments, with a main feature in its health, relationships, food, and recreation departments?
- **Do the articles have common structural elements?** Is the emphasis on expert research and opinion, or does the magazine prefer more first-person or man-on-the-street reporting?
- **What is the style for most of the articles?** Is the writing chatty and conversational? Objective and more formal? Do the arti-

cles infuse humor into the topic, or are they more matter-of-fact?

- **What other elements are tied into the articles?** Does each main piece include one or two sidebars? Are there photos or illustrations with each piece? Does the magazine use pull quotes to emphasize certain points?

It isn't enough to know what a given magazine covers and who its readers are. If you hope to land an assignment, you also have to know how to present your idea so that it fits the editor's style and taste. You might have a great idea for a first-person travel piece, but if the magazine you're targeting never uses first-person material, you're headed for a rejection. Likewise, submitting a query for a celebrity profile to a magazine that doesn't use them is a waste of time and energy. Use your critical thinking skills on the material in your target magazine to figure out what's likely to hook an editor.

Studying the Readership

Successful magazines have clearly defined profiles of their target readership that cover everything from simple demographic data (age, income, education level, church membership, and so on) to things like purchasing behavior, hobbies and interests, and career aspirations. Everything that appears in the publication, from feature articles and columns right down to the tiny classified ads at the back of the book, is carefully crafted to appeal to one or more aspects of that reader profile. The best idea in the world will be answered with a resounding no if it doesn't serve the needs of a magazine's subscriber base. Yet, amazingly, novice writers sometimes focus so hard on impressing editors that they neglect to study the real market for their work: the reader.

How do you learn who a magazine's readers are? The market directories are a good place to start. The listings often include a brief description of magazines' target readers—working mothers, teenage girls, college-educated technophobes, gaming industry managers, etc. But to really gain an understanding of your potential readership, you have to study more than just the articles in the magazine.

Helpful Hints

If you can, get hold of the magazine's media or advertiser kit. This will include useful information about the magazine's readers, which will help you further refine your article's slant. Sometimes you can find these kits, or at least request them, on the magazine's Web site. Such kits often include a sample issue of the magazine, too.

Look at the Ads

Ads don't make it into magazines by accident. They are placed because the advertiser thinks the magazine's readership matches the product's target consumer. They have to; advertising is expensive, and companies can't afford to throw away money by going after the wrong kind of potential buyer. You probably won't find Harley-Davidson advertising in an issue of *Redbook*, and you probably won't find Pantene advertising in an issue of *Field & Stream*.

The ads, therefore, can give you quite a bit of insight into the mind of your potential reader. If there isn't any liquor advertising, for example, readers probably won't be interested in an article about the resurgence of martini parties. And that means the editor won't be interested, either.

Read the Letters

Many magazines print letters from their readers, and you can glean some interesting information from studying these. What stories or articles prompted readers to write in? What touched a chord with them? Do controversial articles or those with a strong human interest element get the most reaction? What do readers tend to criticize? What do they want more of? Even if you haven't read the articles referred to, the letters can provide valuable clues about what readers want and expect from their publication.

Guidelines for Submission

The ins and outs of magazine publishing are a mystery to most writers, and especially to beginners, who don't understand why it takes so long for editors to respond to even the briefest queries. It's really a simple matter of logistics. The editor you query has dozens of other responsibilities on top of reading and responding to ideas for future articles, and, no matter how well organized the editor is, those other responsibilities will infringe on her schedule for getting things done.

Helpful Hints

Just like book editors and agents, magazine editors get annoyed when writers sidestep the submission guidelines. Don't send a complete manuscript unless it's requested, and don't send e-mail queries if the guidelines specify snail mail only. Following the guidelines is an easy way to promote a good first impression.

This is why editors develop submission guidelines for hopeful writers. Experienced editors develop a sort of sixth sense about what's right and what's wrong for their magazines. For most of them, especially in dealing with nonfiction, a query letter is the only tool they need to make a yes-or-no decision. They also have their own preferences for receiving submissions. Many editors take submissions home to read in the evenings or on weekends, so it's more convenient for them to receive hard copies via regular mail. Also, many of them dislike having their e-mail inboxes clogged with material from unknown writers; they might accept assigned material electronically, but they may not want to have to print out a bunch of e-mail queries.

For fillers and other very short nonfiction pieces, you can include the completed manuscript with a cover letter. But, unless you're writing an article on spec, don't do the work of writing the piece until you get a green light from the editor. For magazines that accept fiction and poetry, many editors want to skip the query stage and see the completed piece. Again, the submission guidelines will tell you how the editor wants to receive material.

How to Craft Your Query

For both book and magazine ideas, the most important piece of writing you'll do is the query letter. For one thing, it's an essential sales tool; ideas gain traction or slide into oblivion based on the query. But, even more important, your query is the only piece of writing that an editor is certain to read. Impress her with your initial letter, and you improve your chances of breaking into print because, even if one idea doesn't go anywhere, editors get a good impression of you from a well-crafted query.

There are lots of books about how to write good query letters, but be careful about copying styles, structures, or formats from these books. Magazine editors get thousands of copycat queries a year lifted directly from such sources, and still most ideas get rejected. Your query letter needs to be inspired by your own ideas and your own words. It also needs to be to the point.

Be Brief

A good query letter is tight. Unless you're pitching a particularly complex idea—and there are very few magazines who are interested in lengthy, complex articles from freelancers—your query letter should fit on one 81/2 × 11 page. The first paragraph is your hook; the second paragraph fleshes out your idea and specifies the length and any other elements, like sidebars and photos. In the third paragraph, give a short summary of your qualifications to write the piece. Close with an appreciation of the editor's time and a call to action: "Thank you for your time and consideration. I look forward to hearing from you." (Sample queries are located in Appendix B.)

Make sure your complete contact information is in your query—name, mailing address including zip code, telephone number including area code, and e-mail address—and always include a SASE so the editor can respond. Editors don't call with rejections; the only way you'll know that you've been turned down is if you include the SASE.

Be Enthusiastic

Enthusiasm is contagious, even from a page of typescript, and so is boredom. Don't fill your query with a lot of hype, but do imbue it with a sense of your own excitement about the idea you're pitching. Editors can tell if you're really interested in the topic or if you're just hoping to get an assignment so you can pay some bills. Not surprisingly, they prefer to work with writers who have some genuine enthusiasm for their assignments.

Accepting Work

When an editor says yes to your query, he'll most likely call you to talk about it. This conversation should cover essentials like word count, the due date, and payment arrangements. You also should talk about the scope of the assignment. Does the editor want sidebars? How many people do you need to interview? Are there other sources the editor wants you to include? Does the editor want to adjust the slant or make sure your article covers certain information? Getting all these things ironed out in the initial phone call can save a lot of aggravation for both of you later on.

Helpful Hints

As a new writer, you can't expect to get the top pay rate; yours may be significantly lower until you prove yourself to the editor. Remember, too, that the rates listed in market directories are only ballpark figures. Some writers get less than the minimum listed, and some established writers get significantly more.

It's also a good idea to clarify the magazine's pay policies. Will you get paid on acceptance, or not until the piece is published? How soon after you turn in your work (or after it's published) can you expect a check? If the editor later decides she can't use your article, will you get a kill fee?

Try, Try, Try Again

The most effective queries are tailored to a specific magazine's readership. If you're thinking that dozens of markets will be interested in your idea, that's a good sign that you haven't refined your slant properly. Ideas that are too broad or vague usually don't appeal to magazine editors, and, in this super-competitive business, no editor wants to publish what every other magazine is publishing.

That said, it is possible to take one idea and break it into viable pieces for two or more potential markets, as long as you make sure the readerships of your intended markets don't overlap. Very few magazines these days are interested in buying simultaneous rights unless the other publications are practically unrelated to their own. A select few will purchase reprint rights, but, even then, you'll probably have to look for non-competing publications. Don't fool yourself into thinking that every one of your target markets will be satisfied with, or even interested in, a rehash of material that you've already had published elsewhere.

The only way to determine whether you can sell the same article twice is to scour the market listings and submission guidelines. Don't waste your time or energy pitching reprint or simultaneous rights to markets that don't accept them. Instead, focus on refining your idea for one or two specific markets.

Chapter 6

The Basics of Book Proposals

Find a Target

Some writers have dreams of landing a fat contract from one of the big-name publishers and overlook the realities of the publishing business, not to mention genuine opportunities elsewhere. Just as you have to study the magazine markets to find a good fit for your articles and short stories, you have to study the needs of agents and editors to find those who are most likely to be interested in your book. But matching your material is only part of the process. Ultimately, you want a good publishing experience, and that goes beyond mere dollars-and-cents issues.

What Do You Want to Accomplish?

One of your goals, of course, is to see your name on the cover of a book. But there are other considerations that are just as important, such as working with an agent or editor who shares your vision and enthusiasm for your work. If this is your first book, it might be important for you to find an agent or editor who is willing to be a mentor or coach of sorts, helping you learn the ropes and get over any rough spots. If your novel is more literary than commercial in nature, finding a publisher who will preserve the integrity of your story and style may be more important to you than one who will organize a twenty-city book tour and a major ad campaign.

Thinking beyond the simple fact of getting published takes some soul-searching because you have to identify your priorities. The good news is that you have complete control over deciding what is most important to you. Once you've figured that out, your search for an agent or publisher actually becomes a little easier, because now you know exactly what you're looking for.

Helpful Hints

Most writers have both business projects and personal projects. Business projects are those that you don't necessarily have a passion for, but which will help you attain short- or long-term goals. Personal projects are those you feel strongly about. Your priorities likely will be different for business and personal projects.

Tiered Marketing

As with any other writing project, your marketing plan for your book proposal should be laid out in phases. Do your research and create a list of possible agents or editors you want to query, and then divide your list into at least two groups. The first group consists of the agents or editors who seem to be the best matches for your material, both in terms of fit and of your own priorities. Limit this group to a maximum of six and see what kind of response you get.

Remember that you can query agents simultaneously, or you can query editors simultaneously, but don't mix the two. Many agents won't consider material that already has been marketed to editors, simply because it's difficult (though not impossible) to get editors to reconsider rejected ideas. Your odds of finding an agent diminish greatly if you've already peppered a long list of editors with your query.

If you don't get any requests for your proposal from your first choices, there are two courses of action open to you. You can move on to your second choices, again limiting your second-tier list to no more than six agents or editors. Or you can re-evaluate your query. A well-written, well-targeted query should get some kind of response, even if it's only a note of encouragement or a suggestion for improvement. If your query isn't generating anything but form rejection letters, chances are you'll get the same results from your second choices if you don't make changes.

Helpful Hints

You should prepare your proposal before you send out query letters because you want to be able to fulfill a request for material as soon as possible. If an agent or editor has to wait weeks or months while you put your proposal together, she probably will forget why she was interested, or, worse, lose interest altogether.

You can send out simultaneous queries without announcing to the agents or editors that you are doing so. However, when you get a request for your proposal, be sure to inform the agent or editor in your cover letter that you have queries pending with others. Don't be smug or threatening about it; it's just a courtesy, and it allows you to respond to another request for a proposal with a clear conscience—as long as you tell the second requester that another agent or editor is reviewing your material, too. The disadvantage to sending out simultaneous queries is that an agent or editor may feel pressured to rush consideration of your project, and that can end up shortchanging both of you.

Submitting Your Fiction

Even if you've published short stories or a nonfiction book or two, you'll have to have a complete manuscript before you try to market your novel. Agents and editors generally insist on this, sometimes even for your second or third novel. This is because too many of them have signed contracts with new novelists, only to discover that the writer can't finish the work. In your query, remember to include an exact word count for your manuscript; a phrase like "approximately 125,000 words" will make an agent or editor think that you haven't finished the novel, and they'll be less likely to ask for any other materials.

When you get a request for more material, many agents and editors won't ask for the full manuscript. Instead, they'll ask for a synopsis and perhaps the first fifty pages or the first two or three chapters. Only when they've had a chance to review these will they ask to see the entire manuscript.

The Synopsis

A synopsis is a short overview of your story. It should cover all the major plot points, but it shouldn't delve into too much detail. A good synopsis usually runs two to three pages, single-spaced, but it should never be longer than five pages. It is written in the present tense and, ideally, in the same style as your manuscript.

Writers often feel intimidated by the synopsis, because it can feel like you're shortchanging your hard work by condensing it into a few short pages. But it's an important weapon in your marketing arsenal. A good synopsis hooks the reader—the agent or editor—and makes him feel that he has to read the story. Introduce your main characters and give an idea of the setting, but don't go overboard with subplots and twists.

Helpful Hints

Your synopsis must include the ending of your story. Agents and editors will not be tricked into asking for your full manuscript if you omit the ending in your synopsis. On the contrary, they will assume that either you don't know how your story ends or that you are otherwise not ready to be a published author.

Try thinking of your synopsis as a brochure for a cruise. The brochure whets your appetite for travel rather than sating it. It offers intriguing glimpses of the overall experience, but it doesn't try to replicate the actual experience. This is your goal when you write your synopsis. You want to paint an accurate and enticing picture of your story, but agents and editors don't expect (or want) all the rich detail of your story until they read the actual manuscript.

The Outline

Agents and editors sometimes, though not always, will request a chapter-by-chapter outline of your novel. It's a matter of the agent's or editor's personal preference rather than an industry standard. However, it's a good idea to have one prepared in case it is requested.

An outline is really a short synopsis of each chapter, usually two or three sentences long. As in your synopsis, your objective is to highlight the main plot points in each chapter. Write it in the present tense, with chapter numbers and titles, if you elect to use them, in all caps: "In CHAPTER ONE: AT THE AIRPORT, Joe Martin arrives in Los Angeles to spend a weekend with a woman he's been chatting with online but has never met." Your outline should be single-spaced, with an extra line between chapter descriptions.

The Cast of Characters

Like the outline, not all agents and editors expect or ask for a cast of characters. Some do, though, because it can help them keep track of the main players while they're reading your sample chapters. Again, it's useful to have this prepared in case you do get a request for it. All you need is a short paragraph on each of your main characters; you don't need to include minor characters. Give a brief description of each character's motivations and problems that have a direct bearing on your story. Keep each character bio to two or three sentences if possible. Single-space each bio, with an extra line between bios.

Sample Chapters

If an agent or editor likes your query, she'll probably ask for a synopsis and the first two chapters or the first fifty pages of your manuscript. She is not interested in seeing chapters from the middle of your story, or your stirring final chapter. Her goal right now is to see whether your story grabs the reader from the first sentence and keeps him engaged through the opening scenes.

Agents and editors want to see the beginning pages or chapters of novels because first-time novelists often take too long to get to the meat of their stories. By looking at your opening pages, an agent or editor can see whether your manuscript begins where your story really begins.

Submitting Your Nonfiction

Nonfiction books usually are sold on the basis of a proposal rather than a complete manuscript. But, even though you don't have to write the whole book before you begin marketing it, you do have to put substantial time and thought into crafting your proposal. You need to do the same kind of research to find appropriate agents and publishers that you have to do for fiction, and you have to do additional research to show agents and editors that there's a large potential market for your book. You'll find a sample nonfiction proposal in Appendix B. These proposals usually are between thirty-five and fifty pages and consist of the following elements:

- **Cover letter.** Not the same as your query letter. Remind the agent or editor that he asked to see your proposal, include a short paragraph about your book, then close.
- **Table of contents.** For your proposal package, not for your book. It shows the agent or editor what you've included in your package. This will be the last page you prepare for your proposal.
- **Overview.** A broad look at your book in one to three pages. Always written in the present tense. It should also include an approximate word count for your book.
- **Author's bio.** A one-page narrative of who you are and why you're qualified to write this book, including your writing credentials, if any, and other credentials that relate to your topic. Always written in the third person, present tense.
- **Outline.** A chapter-by-chapter look at your book, with one- or two-sentence descriptions of the information covered in each chapter. Should fit on two pages, unless you're planning a very lengthy book.
- **The market for your book.** A one-page look at the potential readership for your book. The more hard numbers you can include here, the better.

- **Competition for your book.** Agents and editors want to see this, because part of your sales pitch is showing how your book is different from the others. Explain how your book is different in terms of target audience, information offered, or the approach.
- **Promotion ideas for your book.** Ideas for what you can do to help promote your book, not what the publisher can or should do. If you have a specific platform you can use to build awareness of and demand for your book, include that here, too.
- **Sample chapter(s).** Submit three sample chapters with your proposal. They don't have to be sequential. Include the chapters that best show off your writing ability and your topic.
- **Endorsements, supporting articles, etc., if applicable.** At the end of your package, include supporting materials that are applicable to this particular project. Don't include other material you've written unless it's related to your book topic. Do include articles from high-profile publications where you were quoted as an expert and endorsements for your book from experts, celebrities, or famous authors.

When considering the market for your book, look for national associations or statistics that correspond to your topic. If your targeted reader is the first-time homebuyer, find out how many people buy their first home in a given year. Assume that only 1 percent of your potential market will actually buy your book. To sell 5,000 copies, your potential readership should be at least 500,000.

Helpful Hints

Take care to be objective in your discussion of the competition. If you sound mean, petty, or arrogant, you run the risk of turning off an agent or editor. Besides, the agent or editor might have worked on the book you're criticizing.

Don't panic if you don't have endorsements or articles to append to your proposal; most writers don't, and lots of them manage to get publishing contracts from their proposals anyway. In the end, your work has to stand on its own, and even the most gushing blurb from the most famous writer living won't convince an agent or editor to go ahead with a bad proposal.

Some Elements Are Required

Whether you're writing fiction or nonfiction, every proposal package must include a cover letter, an author's bio, and a SASE. You also might want to include a copy of your original query in your proposal package. It helps to remind the agent or editor why she was interested in your material and saves her the trouble of searching for your original query. Put the query right behind the cover letter.

Cover Letter

The cover letter is a short business letter. Your goal is to remind the agent or editor that he requested your proposal and (very briefly) what your book is about. If there are any new developments pertaining to your book's topic, include that information in your cover letter as well. Close by thanking the agent or editor for his time and interest and say you look forward to hearing from him.

Make sure all your contact information is on your cover letter, including your area code and zip code. If you choose to create your own letterhead, select a style and font that is clean and easily readable. Agents and editors who want to contact you don't want to break out the magnifying glass to decipher your telephone number. *Never* handwrite your cover letter.

About the Author

Agents and editors want to know about your qualifications to write your book, so every proposal must include a short narrative about you. (A sample author's bio is included in Appendix B.) Written in the third person, your bio includes your published credits, your expertise on your book's topic, and any awards you have won that relate to your writing or your book topic. Your education and work experience should be included only if they are related to your book topic, or if they give you a platform for promoting your book.

Helpful Hints

If your book is a collaboration with another author, write an "About the Author" bio for each of you. For nonfiction, if one of you is the expert on the topic and the other is the writer, put the expert's bio first. For fiction, put the authors' bios in the order you want your credit to appear on the book. If you want the credit to read "Jane Smith and Robert Brown," put Jane Smith's bio first.

If you have published credits, put them in the first paragraph; this is the first thing most agents and editors will look for. List book credits first, then magazine and large-circulation newspaper credits. List well-known publications by name. If you don't have credits with big-name periodicals, you can say your "work has been published in several regional and local magazines and newspapers." If you don't have any published credits to include, do not call attention to that in your bio. Instead, find a way to incorporate your life experience and accomplishments into a positive reflection of your writing ability.

SASE

Most proposals should fit in a 9 × 12 or 10 × 14 mailer. For your SASE, include the same-sized mailer, with postage affixed, the agent's or editor's name and address in the upper left corner, and your name and address in the center. This is important—and too often forgotten by writers—because some agents and editors separate SASEs from proposal pages. Fold your return mailer in half and place it directly underneath your cover letter.

Some writers prefer to send their proposals via a shipping service like UPS or FedEx because they can track deliveries easily, although the U.S. Postal Service now offers tracking services without requiring the recipient to sign for your package. If you use a service other than the regular mail, don't expect the agent or editor to return your proposal the same way. It's just far too cumbersome, what with special labels and account numbers and finding a drop box or calling for pick-up service. It's easier on everyone if you just include a regular, stamped mailer for returns, no matter which shipping method you use.

Only Give Your Best

When you send out your proposal, you're still in the courting stage of your relationship with an agent or editor. Just as you would be on your best behavior for a first date or a job interview, you need to present your best in your proposal. Of course, the main thing agents and editors look for is outstanding content, but a clean, professional appearance gives your outstanding content the best background possible.

Format and Mechanics

Agents and editors spend many long hours reading thousands and thousands of pages of typescript, and you can imagine how tired their eyes get. You can make their job a little easier by making sure you follow standard formatting practices for your submission. Synopses for fiction and overviews and discussions of market, competition, and promotion ideas can be single-spaced, as can your author's bio. Sample chapters should always be double-spaced, and each chapter should begin on a fresh page with a three-inch top margin. All other pages should have one-inch margins all around.

Don't bind your proposal; agents and editors prefer loose pages. Because of this, you need to take precautions in case your pages get scattered by an accidental bump against the agent's or editor's desk at work or an affectionate pet on the couch at home. Each page of your proposal, beginning with your synopsis or overview, should have a header with the page number in the upper right corner and either your last name or the title of your book in the upper left corner.

Helpful Hints

Never send out the only copy of your material, whether it's a query letter, proposal, or manuscript. Keep an extra hard copy for your files and store a backup copy on your computer or a disk. If you have more than one copy, you won't have to insure your proposal when you ship it out or fret about getting it back.

Finally, double-check your spelling, punctuation, and grammar. Remember, you're trying to impress an agent or editor with your writing, so mechanics count. If your word-processing program has a spelling and grammar check, use it, but keep in mind that these programs have limitations when it comes to correct word usage. Complex sentence structure also can confuse these programs. If spelling, punctuation, and grammar aren't your strong suits, find someone who is good at these things to proofread your copy and keep a good dictionary and style guide handy.

Double-Check Your Package

Professional authors often make a checklist for each proposal they send out, just to make sure they don't forget anything. Your checklist might include the elements of your proposal package, discussed above, as well as more mundane things, such as ensuring that you've included your own address on your self-addressed, stamped envelope. Always affix the proper postage to your SASE; don't paperclip it or substitute a check for actual stamps. Make sure your phone number includes the area code.

Avoid These Common Mistakes

Beginning writers tend to make the same kinds of mistakes when they start to send out their proposals. You can make your proposal stand out from the crowd—and improve your chances of getting a yes from an agent or editor—by taking the time to do a final spit-and-polish before you drop your package in the mail.

Choose the Right Recipients

Probably the most common complaint from agents and editors is that they get too much material that isn't appropriate for them. No matter how many times they say they do not handle romances, for example, they still get dozens of queries and proposals for romance novels every month. It's almost as if these writers don't read the submission guidelines; they seem to just pull names and addresses out of the agents' and publishers' directories at random.

If you want to be successful in your quest for publication, you must give agents and editors what they want. These days, with so many directories that specify what they're looking for and what they're interested in, and often Web sites that give aspiring writers this same essential information, there is really no excuse for wasting your time and theirs by sending stuff they don't want. The good news is that, if you do your homework, you have a much better chance of finding an agent or editor who loves your work and can't wait to get you signed up.

Know Your Purpose

A proposal is a sales tool; your objective is to sell an agent or editor on your book. That means you have to give them enough information to make a decision. Omitting key information, such as a synopsis (complete with the ending) of your novel or the discussion of competing books for your nonfiction book, defeats your purpose. At best, it delays the decision-making process, because the agent or editor has to ask you for the missing information. At worst, the agent or editor may decide to pass on your project because your proposal is incomplete.

You might find it hard to believe, but some hopeful writers forget to include their contact information in their proposals. It's pretty frustrating for an agent or editor to read a proposal that is exactly what she has been looking for, only to find that the writer has given his name but no mailing address, telephone number, or e-mail address.

Stay Positive

Addison Mizner, a flamboyant self-taught architect who designed many of the most extravagant homes in Florida during the early twentieth century, once said that misery loves company, but company does not reciprocate. In other words, even if you've collected several rejections and are feeling discouraged, don't let that color your communications with the people who remain on your marketing list. If you aren't enthusiastic about your proposal, you're going to have trouble generating enthusiasm in publishing professionals.

It can be difficult, but each time you send your proposal to an agent or editor, you have to project an image of cheerful confidence. Don't mention how many times your proposal has been rejected or how you feel about the people who rejected it. After all, even if you haven't gotten an offer yet, you still believe in your work, and each new contact is a clean slate. Let that be the sense you convey every time you send your proposal out.

Follow Directions

Few things are more annoying to agents and editors than hopeful writers who can't or won't follow instructions. Like most of us, agents and editors have particular tastes about what they want to see. If you don't get specific instructions about what to send, follow the guidelines in this chapter; that way, you'll be sure to include everything they need without overloading them.

If you do get specific instructions, adhere to them as closely as you can. Some agents and editors want only to see the synopsis and first chapter of your novel. Others might want the synopsis and the first three chapters. More is not always better, and inundating an agent or editor with unwanted paper is not the way to win her good graces. Don't send four chapters when she asks for two and never tell her she has to read your entire manuscript to appreciate it. She's a pro; she knows what she needs and will ask for it.

A few might request an outline of your novel as well. Be prepared to supply what they ask for, and do it graciously. Even if you've already sent a synopsis, send another copy. Remember that the request is a sign of interest, and that's always a good thing.

Chapter 7

Submission Protocol

Query First

The query letter is the first line of defense for agents and editors who are trying to stem the flood of paper, or at least maintain some semblance of control over it. Even those who will read unsolicited proposals and manuscripts usually prefer a query first. Queries are convenient for agents and editors to read; well-crafted queries make it easy for them to decide whether they want to see more. In fact, queries are such good prescreening tools that many agents and editors won't accept anything but a query in the first stage of marketing. That way, they don't spend valuable time dealing with stacks of material that isn't right for them.

Helpful Hints

Telephone queries are not appropriate until you're well-established with an agent or editor, and even then you shouldn't do it often. A phone call is never appropriate when you're first contacting agents or editors; they are extremely busy with existing clients and works in progress, and phone calls from hopeful unknowns are annoying and intrusive.

Many writers don't like queries and would just as soon skip this step in the process. This may be because writers are impatient to get their work into the hands of the people who can help them get published, or it may be because many writers haven't learned how to write effective query letters. But there are distinct advantages to mastering the query, and it isn't as difficult as you might think.

The Advantage of Queries

There are three good reasons to query before you send out your book proposal, short story, or article.

First, if you read the market listings carefully, you'll notice that response times for queries typically are much shorter than response times for proposals and manuscripts. It's simple logistics: It takes less time to read a one-page letter than it does to read a fifty-page proposal or a four-hundred-page manuscript, and the faster the agent or editor reads your material, the more quickly he can get back to you.

Second, when an agent or editor asks for your material based on your query, it means you've captured his interest. It may seem like a slim advantage, but, in the highly competitive publishing business, it's better to have an agent or editor looking forward to receiving your package rather than glancing through your pages to see if it's worth his time to read it.

Third, querying first saves you money. A one-page query letter with SASE costs you two first-class stamps. A fifty-page proposal with a stamped return mailer will cost you at least a few dollars to mail, and more if you choose to use a shipping service like UPS or FedEx. It may not seem like a huge difference, but it can add up quickly. Mailing ten query letters will cost you less than $10. Mailing ten proposals can cost $40 or more. The extra $30 might be worth it if you were assured of getting more positive responses, but that isn't the way it works. Save your money and save your proposal for the agents and editors who ask to see it.

Helpful Hints

An agent or editor who isn't interested in your current project may keep your name on file for future projects. It's not a guarantee by any means, but agents and editors often keep notes about the particular qualifications of would-be authors, and they might go through those notes when they need someone with just those qualifications.

Crafting a Good Query

Your query letter may well be the most important piece of writing you ever do, because it's the one thing you can be sure an agent or editor will read, and he will decide whether to request more based solely on your query. Your objective, then, is to convince him that you have the perfect article or book idea for him, one that he would be crazy to pass up, and that you are the perfect person to write your idea. And, as a general rule, you should be able to convince him in one page.

The first paragraph of your query is the hook; you have to interest the agent or editor and make her want to read on. For fiction, you might be able to adapt the opening of your short story or novel. For nonfiction, you can use statistics, summarize an issue, or relate an anecdote to lead into your idea. In the second paragraph, expand on your idea. Offer the title of your article, story, or book, and the word count; you can estimate the word count for nonfiction books, but give a precise count for fiction, especially if you're a first-time novelist.

Helpful Hints

When you query for magazine articles, be sure to specify which rights you're offering for sale. Most magazines purchase first serial rights, which means the work hasn't been published anywhere else, including on the Internet. Some purchase second serial rights, also known as reprint rights. If you have photos or illustrations for your article, mention that in your query, too.

In your third paragraph, explain why you're the right person to write your idea. Be sure to include your published credits if you have them. If you don't have any credits to list, focus on your other qualifications to write your project, such as expertise on the topic.

Close with an acknowledgement of the recipient's time and a call to action. The standard, two-sentence closing found in most business letters works perfectly for your query letter: "Thank you for your time and consideration. I look forward to hearing from you."

Remember that you must include a self-addressed, stamped envelope with your query if you hope to get a response. Although agents and editors who are interested in your work might call you to request more material, they are just as likely to write a short letter specifying what they want to see next. However, they can't do that if you neglect to include an SASE.

Understand the Guidelines

One of the most common complaints agents and editors have about dealing with hopeful writers is the extraordinary number of inappropriate submissions they receive. On their bad days, agents and editors may feel that writers blindfold themselves, open one of the various directories at random, stab a page with a pushpin and send their materials to whichever name is closest to the pin. Indeed, there seems to be no other explanation for fiction submissions to agents and editors who only handle nonfiction, or pitches for relationship articles to magazines that cover, say, aviation.

Agents and editors include their listings in the directories so writers will know what they're interested in, how they prefer to be contacted, and other essential information. Many of them also publish this information on their Web sites. With these resources at your disposal, there really is no excuse for poorly targeting your submissions.

Genre First

Sometimes writers do their research backward, looking first for agents or editors who will accept unsolicited proposals or manuscripts, for instance, because they don't want to mess around with a query letter. Now that you know the advantages of the query process, though, the first thing you should always look for is an agent or editor who handles your type of work. If a magazine, literary agency, or book publisher doesn't publish what you're writing, nothing else in the directory listing matters.

Methods of Contact

Directory listings usually are quite explicit about how these publishing professionals prefer to be contacted. Some accept queries only and will not open unsolicited submissions. Some accept proposals or partial manuscripts, and some will consider complete manuscripts. When a listing says something like, "Queries preferred, but accepts proposals," you should follow the preferred method.

With the proliferation of home computers and e-mail, listings now usually state whether the agent or editor accepts electronic submissions. Again, pay attention to preferences. Some agents and editors may prefer e-mail queries, but that is by no means universal (and it doesn't necessarily mean a faster response time, since they still have to read through dozens, if not hundreds, of submissions every week). If e-mail is not specifically listed as the preference, use regular mail to submit your material. You won't lose much time, and, since so much submission reading is done after business hours, most agents and editors still prefer to have hard copies.

Practice Patience

The picture you have of the publishing world depends on where you're sitting. From the inside, a magazine, literary agency, or publishing house is an busy and active place. Days are crammed with meetings, phone calls, e-mails, questions, crises to be resolved, and decisions of varying importance to be made. There are dozens of tasks to be completed and hundreds of details to be considered, and it all has to be done this month, this week, or this morning.

From the writer's desk, on the other hand, the journey to publication is about as speedy as the flow of sap in February, consisting mainly of long periods of waiting punctuated by tiny drips of activity. You send off your query and wait for a response. You get a request for your proposal, so you send that off, and then you wait for a response. You get a preliminary offer and begin negotiating the terms of the contract, and then you wait for the contract to be approved. Finally, just after you decide your head will explode if you have to wait one more day, you get a phone call saying it's a done deal, and now you have something concrete and specific to work on.

Patience isn't just a virtue for writers. It's a protective shield for your mental health. Especially if you're just starting your writing career, nothing is going to happen quickly from your perspective.

Typical Response Times

Writing is a solitary activity, so it's easy to forget that your work isn't the only thing sitting on an agent's or editor's desk waiting to be reviewed. In fact, your work is among reams of submissions from other writers, each of whom also may be oblivious to the realities of the industry. This is why market directories commonly list average response times.

Helpful Hints

Never call an agent or editor to see if he received your material or what he thinks of it. If you haven't heard anything, it means he either hasn't gotten to it yet or is still considering it. Always assume that no news is good news.

Note that reporting times vary substantially, depending on the establishment and what has been submitted. Most places respond to queries in two to six weeks. It might take two to three months to respond to a proposal. Complete manuscripts have the longest response times, which can range from three months to a year. Note also that the response times (sometimes called "reporting times") are averages. Aside from the daily demands that take precedence over considering new submissions, illness, vacations, and personnel changes can create enormous backlogs.

Marking Time

Did you ever collect cereal box tops when you were a kid so you could send off for a free decoder ring or other prize? Remember how it seemed to take eons for that package to arrive? Writers tend to go through similar agonizing periods of waiting after they've mailed their queries or proposal packages. Days suddenly seem to take forty-eight hours instead of the standard twenty-four, and weeks feel like ten to twelve days.

You can put time back in perspective by keeping track of when you actually mail your submission and when you can reasonably expect to get a response. Keep a calendar especially for this purpose, whether it's in the form of an appointment book, a desk or wall calendar, or the calendar function on your computer. Mark down what you send, where you sent it, and the average response time for that market. When you find yourself getting antsy because you haven't heard anything, a glance at your calendar can tell you whether your anxiousness is premature.

When to Follow Up

What if it's been three months since you sent your query, and you still haven't heard anything? Should you call, e-mail, or write? This can be a tough decision, because you don't want to come across as a pest. Sometimes—not often, but sometimes—queries and other materials do get lost in the bustle of busy offices. Chances are, though, that the writer made some mistake when sending the material. Check your records and see if any of the following apply.

- **Did you forget to include a SASE?** This is the most common reason writers don't hear back on their submissions.
- **Did you send your query by e-mail?** Even valid, nonspam e-mail sometimes doesn't make it to its intended destination. One study indicated that as much as 40 percent of valid e-mail gets lost in transmission, another reason why regular mail is often preferable.
- **Did you address your query to the right person?** Agents and editors often are responsible for specific types of books or

articles, and if you don't send your material to the right person, it may never get passed along.

When you haven't heard back on your query, you have two options. You can assume that the agent or editor isn't interested and move on to the next phase of marketing, or you can resubmit your query along with a short, polite letter explaining that you didn't receive a response the first time. Don't toss accusations or jump to conclusions about why you didn't receive a response; the polite, professional thing to do is to assume that your original submission was lost, without blaming anyone for it. If you choose this route, make sure you include a SASE and double-check the name and address of the person you want to contact. If you sent your first query by e-mail, send your follow-up by regular mail.

Helpful Hints

Queries for short stories and magazine articles sometimes will get filed in the slush pile for weeks or even months while editors decide whether a piece is right for them. Book queries generally get a yes or no as soon as the agent or editor has time to read it; it's quite rare for agencies or publishers to have a "maybe" pile for books.

Can You Make Multiple Submissions?

When you make multiple or simultaneous submissions, you send your article, short story, or book idea to two or more magazines, agents, or publishers at the same time. Directory listings usually specify whether this practice is acceptable, and many markets will consider multiple submissions. Writers often like the efficiency of sending out batches of material and seeing who responds. But, before you get into the habit of doing this, consider all the ramifications.

First Come, First Served

Most writers choose to make multiple submissions because they can reach all their preferred markets at one time, rather than waiting for one market to respond before moving on to the next one. Some envision being in the middle of a bidding war, with two or more potential markets vying for the same material. This sometimes happens with book manuscripts, but only through agents, because the publishers who get involved in book auctions don't accept unagented material.

Multiple submissions for magazine articles are different, because, in most cases, there are only a few publications that are appropriate for a particular topic and slant, and they are usually fiercely competitive, with overlapping readership and advertising markets. Each wants to scoop the others by having an exclusive. These editors typically are not pleased to be part of a simultaneous submission and may reject it on that basis alone.

If your market research indicates that more than half a dozen magazines are appropriate for a particular article, it is likely that you haven't defined the slant and target audience sharply enough. With such a small universe of potential buyers, it is not too much to ask that they be approached one at a time and that you wait an appropriate period before going to the next on the list.

Helpful Hints

You should indicate in your query or cover letter that you are making simultaneous submissions. However, don't insist that an agent or editor rush his decision; chances are you'll simply encourage her to pass on your idea. Even with multiple submissions, expect to wait at least the listed time for a response.

If you do make simultaneous submissions for any piece of your writing, you should adopt a first-come, first-served policy. Agents and editors will expect this, since you've already told them you're making multiple submissions. If you get a positive response from Publisher X and tell him you want to wait until you hear from Publisher Y, chances are you'll lose the sale. You might even earn yourself a little black mark with that particular editor, who won't be eager to consider your next submission.

The Second Buyer

What if you sell your article to Magazine X and get a call the following week from Magazine Y? Chances are that the editor at Magazine Y is going to be pretty annoyed, because you didn't inform him that the article had been picked up elsewhere. If you're going to make multiple submissions, it's your responsibility to let other markets know when your submission is no longer available. All it takes is a quick letter or e-mail to notify them that you've sold your article and are withdrawing it from their consideration. You don't have to give details, but you should not allow them to waste time chasing an article that you've sold to someone else.

Helpful Hints

Make your materials professional. Use a good-quality white paper, a 12-point readable font like Times New Roman, and black ink. Agents and editors spend much of their waking hours reading, so it's important that your materials be easy on the eyes.

What if Magazine Y offers you more money than Magazine X? You're out of luck if you've agreed to sell your article to Magazine X. Even if you've only made a verbal agreement, be sure to keep your word. If you don't, you'll irrevocably burn bridges, and not necessarily just with the editor you stiff. The publishing world is a small community, and word travels. You would be surprised at how fast you can get a bad reputation, and it can follow you for the rest of your career.

When you come up with a good idea for a magazine article, try to think of at least two possible approaches. That way, you'll be prepared when you have two markets interested in your idea; you can sell each nonoverlapping market first serial rights by writing your article twice, each time with a different slant.

When the Answer Is Yes

A successful submission is one that advances you to the next step on the road to publication. For article queries, it means the editor wants to assign your proposed article, and it's time to talk terms. For book queries, that means an agent or editor asks to see more—usually a proposal or partial manuscript, or sometimes the complete manuscript.

For Magazine Articles

Magazine editors usually will call you to discuss your proposed article and the terms of the sale. He may have suggestions for sources or requests for specific information to be included, and he may want to discuss other elements like sidebars and illustrations. He may even want to tweak the slant you proposed. Your responsibility during this conversation is to listen to the editor's needs and make sure you understand what he's looking for. You also should talk about deadlines, delivery methods, and payment arrangements during this phone call. Keep notes about what you discuss and find out how the editor prefers to be contacted with progress reports or problems.

For Book Queries

Positive responses to book queries usually come in the form of a letter or an e-mail, rarely via telephone. Most likely, an agent or editor will ask you to send a synopsis and the beginning pages or chapters of your novel, or a proposal, including sample chapters, for your nonfiction book. Fulfill the request as closely as you can and don't send more than the agent or editor asks for. Remember that these professionals have developed their own efficient systems for determining whether material is right for them. What they ask for is all they need. Remember, too, that a request for more material is not a guarantee of anything. All it means is that the agent or editor is interested enough to see more. Don't jump ahead to contract negotiations or book-signing schedules. Take the process one step at a time.

When the Answer Is No

The only writer who never receives a rejection is the one who never submits his material to agents or editors. Considered in their proper light, rejection slips really are medals for bravery; they prove that you have the courage and confidence to let publishing professionals tell you what they think of your work. The more courage and confidence you have—that is, the more aggressively you pursue publication—the more likely you are to run into the word no.

Whys and Wherefores

Nine times out of ten, you'll receive a standard rejection letter, which says only that your submission "doesn't suit our needs at this time." If you're like most writers, you'll feel frustrated at the lack of specific criticism or information, and you may wonder whether the agent or editor even bothered to read your stuff. It's impossible to know for sure when the only thing that connects a boilerplate rejection letter to you is your name at the top.

Standard rejection letters are frustrating because many of us have a nagging fear that our writing isn't really any good. Sometimes, we think, it almost would be better if an agent or editor came right out and said our writing stinks; then, at least, we would know what to defend. But one-size-fits-all rejections don't even give us that meager comfort, and we're left to imagine all sorts of horrible reasons for that cold, curt "no."

Helpful Hints

You can improve your odds of acceptance by doing your homework on business considerations. Study the markets. Come up with a strong slant or unique approach to make your article or book idea stand out. Pitch your material to agents and editors who are most likely to be interested in it. The extra work you put in on these factors will pay off in fewer rejections.

You may never learn why your material was rejected, but most often it has more to do with the business needs of the agent or editor than with the quality of your work. Maybe the magazine you're pitching already has a similar article in the hopper, or the topic has grown stale from too much coverage. The agent you approached might have heard from publishers that interest in your particular type of book is ebbing. Perhaps the publisher has a related title in its catalog and doesn't want a new book that would compete with it.

These all are business issues that you might not even be aware of and that are beyond your control. When you get a standard rejection, assume these kinds of business reasons constitute the "why and wherefore" of the rejection and focus your energies on what you can control—the quality of your work.

Responding to Rejections

The only time it is appropriate to respond to a rejection is when the agent or editor has offered you suggestions on how to improve your project. You certainly aren't required to respond. But, if you do choose to respond, the only appropriate method is with a short, polite note thanking the agent or editor for his time and advice.

It is never appropriate to respond with anger or insults. In the first place, such a response is unprofessional, and you don't want to make a name for yourself as being difficult to work with. Keep in mind, too, that editors tend to move around within the industry, and they have little difficulty remembering writers who gave them a hard time. Before you fire off a sheet of invective, ask yourself this: Will you be embarrassed to encounter this same agent or editor a year or two from now when you're marketing a new project?

Helpful Hints

Agents and editors use form rejection letters because, too often, they've received nasty responses from writers whose work they've turned down. Most people prefer to avoid confrontations if possible, and bland, nonspecific rejections offer agents and editors some protection because they provide the least fodder for an irate letter or phone call.

Angry responses to rejections also are ungracious. When agents and editors take the time to even consider your work, they are often doing so during their own free time. If they make specific comments, they are sharing their expertise with you, free of charge. Even if you disagree with the suggestions, you should recognize the spirit of generosity behind them.

The steps for submitting written works have been developed to help agents and editors cope with the volume of material they receive. Perceived shortcuts really are unnecessary detours. You can help the process move along smoothly by understanding and following the protocol, even if it isn't quite as fast as you would like.

Chapter 8

Revising Can Get You the Deal

Who Is Your Client?

Publishing works on the principles of supply and demand, just like any other business, and sometimes it's easier to tackle revisions if you think of your relationship with the publishing business this way. Potential markets are your clients, and you are the supplier of goods. Your responsibility is to understand the demands of your clients and give them what they need so they can serve their clients (i.e., their readers, advertisers, etc.). It's like selling fabric to a sewing store. If none of the store's customers buy corduroy, the store isn't going to carry corduroy in its inventory, and it's pointless for you to try to convince the store owner to purchase your corduroy, even if it's of the best quality ever known.

Thinking of your writing this way has several advantages. First, it requires you to think like an editor and develop your ideas with that perspective in mind. Second, it puts rejections on a business, rather than a personal, basis. An editor who can't use your idea is no longer saying you aren't good enough as a writer; he's simply saying that your article or story or book proposal is not in demand at his particular company. Finally, this approach permits you to remove the blinders many writers wear during the submission process, freeing you from the futile task of trying to jam a square peg into a round hole and allowing you instead to look for square holes or ways to shape your idea so it's round, too.

Serving the client doesn't mean you have to subjugate or abandon your own style of writing. It does mean, however, that it is your responsibility to match your goods with the market, and that sometimes means setting your ego and style preferences aside. If your goal is build your clip file, establish long-term relationships with editors, or simply get paid for doing something you love, your primary consideration should be to craft pieces that suit a particular market. Once you make a name for yourself, you'll have more slack to give rein to your own style.

Helpful Hints

This advice applies to your search for an agent, too. Although your goal is to become an agent's client, you'll be more successful in your wooing if you think of a potential agent as the client and work to give her exactly what her market demands.

Coping with Criticism

Hard as this might be for many writers to believe, constructive criticism in a rejection actually is cause for optimism. When an agent or editor gives you specific reasons for rejecting your work, it usually means that you have interested him but not met his market needs. More important, in most cases like this, it's a rare chance at a do-over, because there is an implicit invitation to revise and resubmit your work, or to submit other pieces to this market.

To take advantage of these opportunities when they arise, you have to be able to put a healthy emotional distance between you and your writing so you can look at it as objectively as possible. Part of doing this involves learning how to weigh and measure criticism. You should be able to discern between helpful and unhelpful comments; helpful ones cite specific issues or problems to be addressed (though not necessarily how to address them), while unhelpful ones are vague and sometimes unkind.

There is no need to respond to a form rejection letter unless the agent or editor has taken the time to jot a personal note at the end of it. Even when you do get such notes, you aren't required to respond. If you choose to respond, though, the appropriate and professional thing to do is to write a brief note or e-mail, thanking the agent or editor for his comments. Never berate him for offering advice, and don't argue about the merits of his comments. You may want to submit work to this person again, and you don't want to tarnish your image. Remember, too, that such comments are a generous donation of the agent's or editor's time and expertise; accept them in a like spirit.

Keep in mind that agents and editors generally won't give specific comments when material just isn't right for them. If you haven't done your market research—that is, if you're sending a techno-thriller to an agent who only handles women's fiction, or a skydiving article to a cycling magazine—chances are you'll get a standard "doesn't suit our needs" rejection letter.

Common Nonfiction Criticisms

Nonfiction criticisms tend to fall into three broad categories: stale ideas, lack of authority, and lack of human interest. The problem, especially for new writers, is that agents and editors don't always define what they mean by these comments. And you can't fix it if you don't really understand what's broken.

Staleness

One of the most common complaints agents and editors have about the submissions they receive is that there's nothing new, fresh, or original. This can be intimidating to new writers, who wonder nervously how they can possibly come up with fresh ideas when people have been exchanging and publishing ideas for thousands of years. If there really is nothing new under the sun, why do agents and editors keep demanding something new?

Here's what these "demanding" agents and editors really mean: They want a fresh perspective on well-worn topics. As discussed earlier, the quickest way to an agent's or editor's yes file is to find and fill a hole in the market. Say you want to write a piece for a travel magazine on the increasing popularity of heritage tourism. This trend has been covered extensively in both trade and consumer magazines, and they aren't likely to be interested in yet another bland look at it. But, if the coverage has overlooked how smaller, lesser-known attractions have been affected by the trend, you've got a brand-new approach to a not-at-all-new topic.

Helpful Hints

You can get new information for an article by contacting the sources you find in already-published articles. If you have questions that those articles didn't answer, ask those questions of the original source. Also ask who else you could contact. Very often, experts will direct you to colleagues who might add another dimension to your coverage.

Lacking Authority

Another common complaint for nonfiction articles and book proposals is that they lack authority. This could mean several things. It may mean that it relies too heavily on one or two experts, or that it doesn't distinguish between opinion and established fact. It also may mean that there are unsupported leaps of logic. These deficiencies almost always are fixable, but it takes some work in the form of additional research and, often, reorganizing the piece to accommodate the changes.

Lack of Human Interest

Finally, agents and editors often complain a nonfiction piece is "flat" or "dry." This usually happens when writers fail to put a human face on an issue. For example, if you're writing an article about the National Flood Insurance Program and delays in getting flood aid to stricken communities, you risk boring your readers to death unless you include the stories of people who are affected by the delays. Unless your target publication is aimed at bureaucrats, a process-y article that quotes only government officials and ignores what most editors call "real people" isn't going to interest anybody.

Common Fiction Criticisms

In fiction, rejection is sometimes as much a matter of taste as of objective standards, and it is especially important for fiction writers to remember that a rejection reflects just one person's opinion. The editor at Magazine G might not like your short story, but the editor at Magazine H might think it's the best thing she has read since Hemingway. That said, there are some common problems agents and editors run across in fiction of any length.

Characterization Issues

Lots of unpublished fiction suffers from one-dimensional characterization. This is a particularly challenging problem for short story writers, because you're limited in the space you have to develop your characters. But agents and editors typically will reject stories with characters who are either too good or too bad to be true. Everyone, even your hero and villain, has both admirable traits and flaws, and your job as a writer is to craft word portraits that reveal the shades of gray among the black-and-white outlines.

So-called "wooden characters" also seriously damage a good story, usually by speaking in stilted, awkward dialogue. Train your writing ear to pick up on and replicate natural patterns of speech, and understand your characters well enough to know what kind of phrasing and vocabulary they would use.

Plot Issues

If an agent or editor advises you to scrap the first three or four chapters of your novel, or says you've included too much "back story," it means your story doesn't begin where your manuscript begins. New writers especially tend to ease into their stories as if they were testing the water in the swimming pool with a shrinking toe, but agents and editors—and readers, for that matter—want you to just dive in and get on with it. The back story is useful to the writer to figure out his characters and the build-up of events to the main story, but it almost always is deadly dull to the reader.

There's another pretty good tip-off that you haven't begun your story in the right place. If you feel compelled to tell an agent or editor to be sure to read up to Chapter 12 because that's where it gets really good, you need to seriously edit your manuscript. The real message in a statement like that is that the first eleven chapters are boring, which is sure to put you in the rejection pile.

Helpful Hints

Agents and editors commonly advise new fiction writers to "bring the plot to the foreground." This means you've allowed too much extraneous material to creep into your story. Remember that every scene in a short story, and every chapter in a novel, must advance the plot. Otherwise, you risk losing your reader and earning a rejection slip.

Before submitting your work, take a hard look at the beginning chapters and ask yourself what would happen if you eliminated them. Would the reader still understand what's going on? Would it help build suspense if you doled out the information contained in the early chapters later on? If the answer is yes (and it often is), you can strengthen your writing immeasurably by taking the time to make these changes before you begin your marketing.

Your stories always should have a motif or theme that weaves through your plot, and your plot progression must make logical sense. If you have to resort to coincidence or other contrivances to bring your story to a climax, consider reworking your plot; readers generally dislike these kinds of stories, and editors won't buy them. Keep narration and exposition to a minimum, and allow your characters to advance your plot through action and dialogue.

Style and Tone Issues

Every writer who has ever taken an English class has been admonished to "show, don't tell" what happens in a story. If your story sounds more like a report on the evening news, you've fallen back on telling readers what they need to know rather than showing them. Think in terms of mystery stories here. The writer knows who committed the crime, but the characters in the story don't know until the end. Readers want to go along with the characters to find out what happens, and they want to make their own judgments along the way by paying attention to the clues you provide in plot and character.

Another common criticism fiction writers hear is that their work is too preachy. This doesn't mean your stories can't take on social or political issues, or that you should shy away from plots that involve controversial topics. However, whatever the lesson, moral, or point of view you're trying to present, you have to allow the reader to absorb it from the momentum of your story. Don't stop the action to expound on your own views. Let your characters and plot work together to get the message across.

Melodrama also often will earn a rejection, unless it's an integral part of the story concept. Even then, stories that blatantly attempt to draw readers in with an exaggerated play on emotion turn off many readers—and therefore many agents and editors. If your work is being described as too sentimental, saccharine, or heavy-handed, this may be why.

Accepting the Challenge

We called rejection slips medals for bravery because they prove you have the courage to submit your work and let others tell you whether it has any market value. Just as important as that medal, however, is what you do after you receive it. In that context, a rejection slip is really a challenge to you to try again.

Assuming that you don't want to stick your work in a drawer and give up your dream of becoming a published writer, you have essentially two options in responding to such a challenge. You can shrug off the rejection from one market and send the material out to the next one on your "possibles" list. Or you can rework your submission to make it more appealing to the markets you want to reach.

New Markets

Many writers elect to move on to the next market on their list, waving a rejection aside with a philosophical, "Oh, well." There's nothing wrong with that approach. In fact, the more philosophical you can be in dealing with rejection, the less stressful your writing career will be. Besides, it's fairly common for your first choice to turn you down, especially if you're aiming at the big markets; they are notoriously difficult to break into.

Helpful Hints

If an agent or editor rejects your current submission but invites you to submit to her in the future, take it seriously. Agents and editors never include this sort of note out of the goodness of their hearts. When they do, it means that they see talent and potential in you, and they want to see more of your work.

If you're collecting rejections further down your marketing list, however, it's likely that there's a serious flaw in your submission. A fistful of form rejections with no personal notes from an agent or editor indicates that your material isn't properly slanted for the markets you're targeting. If you are getting personalized comments, pay attention to them. These are free, professional opinions, and, even if they sting a little, you should treasure them because few writers ever receive them.

Making Changes

The first thing to remember when you're wavering over whether to revise your material is that it is always your decision. Even if a dozen agents or editors have suggested the same changes, you never have to make them if you don't want to. Of course, if you don't make changes, you may not see this particular piece published, but it's your work, and only you can decide whether the cost of making changes outweighs the benefits.

If you do decide to make changes, and if the changes are inspired by comments you received from agents or editors, you should resubmit your revised material to those people first. It's professional courtesy, because these people gave you the benefit of their expertise and experience at no charge, and they most likely did it on their own time. In addition, an agent or editor who is interested enough to offer you advice gives you a subtle advantage over the dozens or even hundreds of other submissions on his desk.

When you do accept the challenge, keep your expectations realistic. If you get a positive response to your query or proposal—that is, an agent or editor asks to see more—don't expect detailed feedback on the material you first submitted. The fact that an agent or editor wants to see more is a good thing. It means your material shows promise; if it didn't, they wouldn't ask for anything else. Demanding an evaluation or critique before you send more material is no way to endear yourself to the professionals in publishing. Keep an open mind and an optimistic outlook, but don't expect to rule the world.

Chapter 9

Contract Negotiations

Types of Rights

A copyright is really a generic umbrella covering a broad spectrum of individual rights. In your contract, you transfer to the publisher some or all of the rights covered under your copyright. The rights you grant will vary depending on the type of work you're selling and who is purchasing it. They can be limited by language, geography, or time, and sometimes by all three.

Serial Rights

Serial rights are sold to periodicals—i.e., newspapers and magazines. Many periodicals purchase only first serial rights, meaning they want to be the first to publish the material. Serial rights can be given on a worldwide basis or restricted to a certain region. Many magazines purchase first North American serial rights, which cover the United States, Canada, and Mexico; some purchase first U.S. serial rights. If the first serial rights aren't specifically limited to a particular geographic area, they cover the world. If first serial rights are limited to the United States or North America, you can sell foreign serial rights to publishers in other countries (except Canada and Mexico, if you've already sold first North American serial rights).

Helpful Hints

To qualify for first serial rights, including syndicated first serial rights, book excerpts must be published before the book itself is published. Excerpts that are published after the book is on the market can only be sold as second serial rights.

Second serial rights, also known as reprint rights, are for subsequent publishers of the same material. If your book on parenting is excerpted in *Parenting* magazine, for example, the magazine is buying second serial rights—also called excerpt or reprint rights. In this case, the excerpt will include a notice about your book, which often helps promote sales. Pay rates for second serial rights are lower than for first serial rights and are often based on a percentage, usually 50 percent, of the rate for first serial rights.

Newspapers sometimes purchase syndication rights, which are a special breed of serial rights. Major U.S. newspaper publishers own papers in several markets and usually have their own wire services through which they distribute articles and features among the member papers. Gannett, for example, owns *USA Today*, as well as dozens of local and regional newspapers around the country. Gannett might purchase syndicated serial rights for excerpts of a book to be published in all its newspapers.

Simultaneous Rights

It's possible to sell the same piece at the same time to two noncompeting markets, although it isn't very common. Because the publishing industry is so competitive, editors rarely are interested in publishing an article or short story that will appear in another publication. And, if you've slanted your article precisely enough, chances are slim that you'll find two markets that want to publish exactly the same piece. However, sometimes a publisher that owns several magazines will purchase one article or short story to appear in more than one of those publications. As noted earlier, make sure you notify editors that you are making simultaneous submissions when you're marketing your work.

Subsidiary Rights

When you sell a book to a publisher, the contract usually will discuss subsidiary rights as well as book-publishing rights. These can include serial and foreign rights, translation rights, movie and television rights, commercial licensing rights, audio books, and special formats, such as Braille or large-print books, or book-club editions. The contract will spell out which rights you give to the publisher and how you and the publisher will split the proceeds.

Some writers want to hang on to all subsidiary rights, thinking they are protecting their future earnings. But major publishers may be in a better position to exploit these rights, and they may insist on the ability to do so, particularly with an unknown author. As long as the earning splits are reasonable, there's no reason why you shouldn't grant these rights to the publisher, provided the publisher intends to actively pursue them.

Splits for these rights will differ depending on the type of right. According to the Authors Guild, an advocacy group for writers, authors should expect to receive 50 percent of the earnings for book club sales and for paperback sales, if the publisher is first publishing the book as a hardcover. The split on movie and television rights can range from a straight fifty-fifty arrangement to a division that heavily favors the author. For nonfiction, foreign rights usually aren't very lucrative; for fiction, though, foreign sales can bring you a lot of money, and you or your agent should try to retain them if you can.

Helpful Hints

There's a difference between foreign rights and translation rights. A publisher may sell your English-language book in France, for instance. The publisher also may sell French translation rights to another company. You should receive 75 percent of the proceeds when your publisher sells translation rights.

Movie, television, and dramatic rights—i.e., for a play—often are sold as an option first, which is a guarantee that no one else can purchase those rights for a specified period. Options fetch a percentage of the total price of the right being optioned; if the movie rights are worth $100,000, for instance, a six-month option might be sold for 25 percent, or $25,000. At the end of the six months (or whatever period is agreed to), the rights revert to the author or publisher, unless the purchaser pays the balance ($75,000 in this example) or renews the option. Whatever the case, the up-front money paid for the option is nonrefundable; the buyer is paying you to "hold" the project, or take it off the market, while he sets up deals with producers, etc. If he decides not to pick up the option, you keep whatever he originally paid for it.

The Authors Guild argues that authors should receive 90 percent of earnings from the sale of television and movie rights. However, many publishers insist on a fifty-fifty split, reasoning that strong sales of the book add significant value to such rights. You should always receive at least 50 percent of such earnings.

Consider the Sale

Which rights are for sale depends on the type of work you're selling and who you're selling to. Magazines generally purchase limited rights, such as first serial rights or one-time rights, but occasionally you'll run across one that purchases all rights. As discussed above, book publishers typically purchase a range of rights, with the advance and royalties for the book itself spelled out and a split between author and publisher specified for subsidiary rights. If you're a stringer for a newspaper, your contributions generally are considered "work made for hire," and the newspaper retains all rights to the material. Any contract for publishing of your work must include the following:

- A description of the work being purchased.
- A specific listing of which rights are being licensed to, or purchased by, the publisher.
- A definition of the rights license period, i.e., how long the publisher owns the rights you are selling and when those rights revert to you.
- Delivery dates for all or portions of the work.
- Terms of payment for the work.

Most publishing contracts will include several other clauses covering such things as acceptability standards, noncompete agreements, and which state laws come into play in the event of a legal dispute between you and the publisher. These clauses usually are part of a publisher's boilerplate, or standard, contract and are not negotiable. Nearly every publisher these days insists on an acceptability or satisfactory clause, which in essence gives them the right not to publish work that doesn't live up to the promises made by the writer.

Noncompete clauses also are the norm; publishers want to make sure their writers don't sell other pieces (articles, short stories, or books) to competing publishers, because such sales could diminish the value of the material they're buying. The "governing law" clause also is a non-negotiable item, because it has to be the state in which the contract is generated—that is, the home state of the publisher or agent.

Description of the Work

The description of the work being purchased can be quite broad or quite specific. In book contracts, the description may be just one sentence, citing the book's working title and its overall focus. Some publishers include the author's outline in the contract, but many don't. Nearly all publishers will include a minimum word count for the manuscript, and some will include a maximum.

Magazine contracts differ, depending on whether you're selling an article or short story that already has been written or being assigned an article that you pitched to an editor. For outright purchases, most magazines offer a simple contract that includes the terms of payment—how much, and when it is to be paid—as well as the title of the piece and the rights being purchased. Such contracts also usually require you to supply your name, contact information, and Social Security number.

In addition to these things, contracts for assigned articles usually will specify the length of the piece and sometimes will even spell out the types of sources to be used. The contract also will have a deadline for completing and delivering the article.

Rights Being Purchased

Unless you agree otherwise in writing, U.S. copyright law states that you are selling only one-time rights to any publisher. This is why even small magazines issue a contract spelling out precisely which rights are being sold and all the other terms of the sale. When you submit your work, whether in a query or with a complete manuscript, you always should specify which rights you are offering for sale.

When you read through the contract, pay close attention to the rights being purchased, because it has a serious impact on how much money you can make from your writing. If you sell all rights to an article or short story, for instance, you cannot resell that piece to anyone else until the rights license period expires. Because of that limitation, you should get more money from a magazine that purchases all rights than a magazine that purchases only first serial rights.

Rights License Period

In book publishing, the rights license period generally lasts as long as the book is in print, and the period covers both the book publishing rights and the subsidiary rights specified in the contract. When the book goes out of print, you usually can regain the rights you transferred by notifying the publisher in writing. To do this, make sure the contract defines "out of print," either by the number of printed copies in stock or the number of sales per year.

Helpful Hints

It is important to have a reversion of rights clause because there may be more money in it for you down the road. If your fourth book becomes a bestseller, it could create demand for your earlier books, and a reprinter might be interested in publishing them again. That means another advance and more royalties on those earlier books for you.

In magazine publishing, you can sell first serial rights only once, unless those rights are limited by geography, language, or other factors. As noted earlier, you can sell first North American or first U.S. serial rights, and then sell first foreign serial rights for the same piece.

Sometimes you can negotiate a set limit on the rights license period for magazines. You can offer first serial rights for twelve months, for example, and if the magazine doesn't publish your piece within that year, the rights revert to you and you can shop them to another magazine.

Delivery Dates

Magazine contracts and many book contracts include one delivery date, or deadline, for the entire manuscript. Some book publishers give interim deadlines, when certain percentages of the manuscript are due, although this is more common for nonfiction books. For most nonfiction books, you'll have at least several months to complete the manuscript. However, when interim deadlines are involved, it's not uncommon to reach the first deadline before you receive the executed copy of your contract.

Helpful Hints

Book authors usually receive free copies of their books when they're published. Typically, hardcover publishers will give authors ten free copies; paperback publishers usually will give twenty to twenty-five. You also will have the option to purchase more copies from the publisher at a discounted rate, which should be specified in your contract.

If you're a first-time or even a second-time novelist, the publisher probably won't offer you a contract until your manuscript is complete; too many publishers have signed fiction writers with unfinished manuscripts who, for whatever reason, were unable to deliver the final product. Also, if a publisher wants major changes to your novel, you most likely will have to make those changes before you get a contract. Because of this now-common requirement for new novelists, your delivery date might be four to six weeks from the signing of the contract. This gives you enough time to put the finishing touches on your manuscript, but not enough to make major changes in your story.

Payment Terms

Your contract should spell out how much you'll get paid for your work and when you'll get paid. This will vary depending on the publisher you're dealing with. If you're stringing for a newspaper, you might get a separate check for each piece, or you may get paid once a month for the pieces that were published in the previous thirty days. Magazines generally pay either on acceptance (which is better for the author) or on publication; because of the long lead times most magazines have, the latter arrangement means you may wait several months before you get paid. Book publishers generally split advance payments into two or more checks, with the first payment made when the contract is executed and later payments tied to delivery of part or all of the manuscript.

Living Up to Your Promise

Contracts are a series of promises between you and a publisher, and it's critical for your reputation and your career as a writer that you keep your end of the bargain. That means delivering your work to deadline, ensuring that your work is your own, and projecting a professional image.

Delivering to Deadline

Deadlines in publishing are not mere suggestions. They are the backbone of a rigorous and highly structured publishing schedule. Most magazines have lead times of two to six months; that means they may start working on the August issue in March or April and the December issue might be put to bed—sent to the printer—as early as June. When writers miss their magazine deadlines, it leaves a hole of sometimes several printed pages in the issue, forcing the editor to search frantically through the slush pile in hopes of finding something appropriate to fill the space. Chances are that editor will not be inclined to give you a future assignment once you've burned him by missing a deadline.

Helpful Hints

If you can't meet a deadline, it is imperative that you let your agent or editor know as soon as possible. If you have an agent, notify her first and let her talk to the editor. Unforeseen circumstances can interfere with your work schedule, and most agents and editors are willing to do what is possible if they are kept abreast of the situation.

Deadlines are just as critical in book publishing. Delivery of the manuscript is just the first step in a hectic process spanning months. Delays in delivery to your acquiring editor means she is delayed in forwarding your manuscript to the development editor, which means delays in getting it to the copy editor, which means delays in getting the final version to the printer. That in turn means a hole in the publisher's catalog and havoc among the sales and marketing staff. And, as in magazine publishing, missed deadlines in book publishing earn you black marks and diminish your marketability for future books.

Original Work

Virtually every contract you encounter in publishing will include a warranties and representations clause, in which you assert that the work you submit is your own material, not plagiarized from any other source, and that it doesn't violate anyone's rights of privacy or other civil rights. Publishers can't take this for granted any more; there have been too many high-profile cases of authors lifting others' material. Most publishers also use various software programs to detect plagiarism, and sometimes this practice is included in the contract so authors know what to expect.

Related to the warranties and representations clause is the acceptability or satisfactory clause, which allows a publisher to reject work that isn't acceptable. Again, this now-standard clause resulted from too many cases where what was turned in was not what the publisher expected. The terms "satisfactory" and "acceptable" may or may not be precisely defined in the contract, but the procedure for fixing problems should be. Generally, the publisher should be required to give you specific reasons for deeming your work unacceptable, citing specific problems that need to be addressed. You should have at least thirty days to correct these specific problems. If you are unable or unwilling to do this, the publisher can hire someone else to make the changes and charge the expense to your advance, or cancel the project altogether. If the project is canceled, you may be required to repay any money you've already received from the publisher.

Professional Image

Not surprisingly, agents and editors prefer to work with writers who are both talented and professional. Professionalism goes beyond meeting your contractual obligations, though. It means working with your agent or editor to resolve problems, handling criticism with at least the appearance of aplomb (however you may feel about it privately), and being respectful of the agent's or editor's time. Phone calls should be kept to a minimum, and e-mails should be limited to necessary communications. Professionalism also means understanding and following the agent's or editor's submission guidelines and being sure to include the SASE with appropriate postage.

Working for Hire

Work-for-hire arrangements, also called works made for hire, are common in newspaper publishing and have become more common in book publishing in recent years. Some writer advocacy groups dislike these arrangements because the writer doesn't retain any rights in the material he creates, so profits are limited. However, works for hire can offer good break-in opportunities for new writers who are building their credentials and clip files.

Under U.S. copyright law, work for hire covers material created by an employee when that work is part of the employee's regular duties, such as a staff writer for a newspaper or magazine. Stringers for newspapers—especially those who cover specific beats, like high school sports or local business—usually are considered independent contractors and fall under the same work-for-hire rules, unless there is a written contract stating otherwise. In all other circumstances, courts have ruled that a valid work-for-hire arrangement requires a written contract in which both parties "expressly agree" to these special terms.

Helpful Hints

Selling "all rights" to an article or story is not the same as doing a work made for hire. U.S. copyright laws allow you to regain your copyright in an "all rights" work after thirty-five years by following established procedures. Rights in a work made for hire stay with the publisher who commissioned the work forever.

In every work made for hire, you'll be paid a flat fee for creating the work. You won't get any royalties, in the case of a work-for-hire book, and you won't be able to sell reprint or any other subsidiary rights, in the case of a magazine or newspaper article. However, if the fee for doing the work is fair, and if you get authorship credit, works for hire can be a lucrative way to build your portfolio and your reputation as a writer.

Getting Credit

From the point of view of most agents and editors, an unpublished author is a liability. You are an unknown quantity, with no name recognition and no demonstrable track record of being able to deliver quality text to deadline. This is why so many publishing professionals insist on published credits. Especially in book publishing, the enormous cost of printing and distributing a new title makes most publishers leery of taking a chance on an untried writer.

There are countless opportunities for freelance writers to earn quite respectable fees for their work—writing advertising and brochure copy, annual reports, speeches, and other pieces for businesses, for example—but these usually don't give you a byline. For new writers who envision careers as book authors or regular contributors to major magazines, the most important factor in getting published—even more important than how much you get paid, or getting paid at all—is getting credit for what you've written. Many magazines and book publishers refuse to work with unpublished writers, so it's critical to your career to build the credentials that will allow you to break into the bigger markets.

For most aspiring writers, the path to the big-time in publishing begins at small-circulation newspapers and magazines, with correspondingly small paychecks. Bylined clips from local newspapers can lead to assignments from larger, regional newspapers; those from small trade or literary magazines can be the first rung on the ladder to publication in progressively larger-circulation and higher-profile magazines. And that collection of clips can provide a springboard into book publishing.

Other opportunities for aspiring book authors include works for hire and coauthorship arrangements. As long as you get authorship credit, a work-for-hire book is exactly the same as a royalty-paying book in the eyes of potential publishers; it proves that you are capable of writing and delivering book-length text. The same goes for coauthorship arrangements. Again, as long as your name appears on the book cover, it counts as a credit and carries the same heft as sole authorship.

Different Types of Payment Arrangements

As noted earlier, the bottom line of any contract is how much you get paid for your work and when you get paid. Obviously, the best arrangement is to get paid when an editor accepts your article or manuscript, but that isn't always the norm, especially among smaller publishing outlets. Before you sign a contract—and before you start spending the money—be clear on when you can expect a check.

"On Acceptance" vs. "On Publication"

Some magazines, and even a few book publishers, delay payment until a piece is actually published, which can leave you hanging for months on end. Most monthly magazines have lead times of two to six months, while it can take up to two years for a book to reach store shelves. The publishers who have payment-on-publication policies usually won't change them, and most established writers choose not to deal with them. Once you've built a respectable clip file, you may want to steer clear of these publishers, too.

Even with payment on acceptance, don't expect a check by return mail. Most publishers will first send out a contract for your signature. You send it back to the publisher, where it is signed by the appropriate person and payment is then authorized, which can take thirty days or longer. You should receive your check with a copy of the executed contract or soon thereafter.

Helpful Hints

Small magazines, including literary magazines, often pay contributors only in copies of the issue in which your article or story appeared. The number of copies you receive usually is between one and five. Directory listings of magazines will indicate "contributor copies" in the payment section.

Kill Fees

Many magazines offer kill fees for articles that have been assigned, but which have been pulled from the publishing calendar for some reason (not related to the writer's work). This could happen for a number of reasons: The editor might decide the topic no longer fits the publication's editorial policy, or a new editor may not like the idea, for example. Kill fees usually are a percentage—sometimes as much as 50 percent—of the fee that would have been paid if the article had been published as planned and are meant to compensate writers for the time they've spent on an assignment that fizzles out.

Helpful Hints

Sometimes writers will be paid for completed articles or short stories that are never published. First send a polite note to the editor, asking when your piece will appear. If it still hasn't been published after a year, advise the editor that you're reclaiming all rights to the piece under the guidelines established by the American Society of Journalists and Authors.

Although the term "kill fee" is rarely used in book publishing, most houses have a similar payment policy when they decide not to publish a manuscript that has been contracted and accepted. Under such circumstances, the author usually is entitled to keep whatever advance payments she has received for the manuscript. All rights in the manuscript should revert to the author once the publisher has decided not to go ahead.

Royalty Payments

The term royalty is hundreds of years old and stems from the practice of monarchs granting special licenses to companies and individuals. These licenses typically transferred control of some natural resource from the king or queen to the licensee, and the licensee often paid the monarch a share of the profits from such resources.

Traditional book publishers, as well as some self-publishing outfits, pay authors royalties, which is a percentage of a book's selling price. Royalties can be based on the list or retail price of a book, or on the wholesale price—typically about half the list price. Advances are paid against future royalty earnings, and advances have to be earned back before the author gets any royalty checks. If the book doesn't sell well enough to cover the advance, you won't get royalty payments.

Say you've negotiated a 10 percent royalty on the list price for your book, which sells for $25. That means you earn $2.50 for every book sold. If your advance is $5,000, you won't earn any royalties until 2,000 copies of your book have sold ($5,000 divided by $2.50 = 2,000).

Most publishers calculate royalties twice a year, and it can take up to ninety days after the end of the royalty period for you to receive a statement. If you've earned royalties during the period, a check will accompany the statement. If not, you'll simply receive the statement, showing how many copies of your book sold during the covered period.

Many publishers allow their authors to audit their royalty statements once a year. This is done at your own expense and involves hiring an accountant to review the publisher's records. Such audits can be quite costly and usually are not warranted unless there is some major discrepancy in sales reports.

Publishing contracts can be fairly simple or remarkably complex, depending on the type of work and the circumstances surrounding it. If you have an agent (who typically only will work on book contracts), he should be familiar with industry standards and represent your best short- and long-term interests in the negotiations. If you don't have an agent, or if you are selling your work primarily to markets where an agent isn't necessary or appropriate, you should consider hiring an attorney experienced in working with authors to review any contract before you sign it.

Chapter 10

Collaborate with Your Editor

The Job of an Editor

Beginning writers often expect editors to be at their beck and call; after all, an editor's job is to support her writers with suggestions and encouragement, right? Well, yes, but that's only a tiny fraction of a typical editor's duties. You might think that your editor is sitting at her desk, idly thumbing through the latest issue of Cosmo and waiting anxiously to hear from you, but the truth is that most editors—even the ones who work for Cosmo—rarely have time to do anything idly.

Meetings, Meetings, and More Meetings

Most editors spend much of their workdays in meetings of one sort or another. There might be an editorial meeting to discuss upcoming magazine issues or potential book projects. Your editor, whether for a magazine or book publisher, probably will meet with the production department several times a week, and maybe even daily, to go over issues with layout, design, and problems with manuscripts. He might meet with the art director or photographer to finalize a book cover, a center spread, or illustrations. And he probably will meet with his boss to discuss contracts for various projects.

In addition, a typical magazine editor may have off-site meetings with advertisers and public relations folks who are trying to get their clients' products placed in the magazine. There may be trade shows or receptions or product demonstrations to attend. He may even have a lunch meeting sandwiched between all the other meetings that make up his day.

Messages, Lots of Messages

In between all the meetings, the editor likely has a stack of phone and e-mail messages that would choke a pig. Some of them are urgent and require her immediate attention—problems with contracts, writers who won't be able to make their deadlines, or any scores of other crises that routinely arise in publishing. Some of them are important but not urgent, such as calls from agents who are checking on the status of submissions or who want to pitch new projects or from established writers who want to do the same.

The bulk of them, though, are ones she can safely push to the bottom of her to-do list, like unsolicited e-mails from unknown writers. These might even get deleted without being opened, depending on what else the editor has on her plate that day or that week.

Reams of Submissions

On top of the meetings and messages, an editor has stacks and stacks of printed material to go through: queries, requested proposals and manuscripts, and all manner of unsolicited packages from hopeful writers. He may try to keep the stacks under control by diligently sorting through the most important ones each day, but it's like trying to hold back a mudslide with a garden hoe. Every day, usually several times a day, drivers from FedEx, UPS, and the U.S. Postal Service dump pound after pound of material on his desk until, by the end of the week, the editor's space looks more like a Mail Boxes Etc. at Christmastime than a professional office.

As part of his job and his efforts at stemming the tide, the editor takes much of this material home with him, with the result that the couch in his living room looks a lot like his desk at work. He spends the bulk of his evening reading through the submissions, deciding which ones will get a rejection letter and which ones merit further consideration. If he's a magazine editor, he may have a third pile, known as the slush pile, for submissions that have him wavering between a yes and a no. Book editors usually don't have slush piles; submissions to them are either rejected immediately or prompt a request for more material. Magazine editors use slush piles as insurance against future problems. If they need to fill a hole in a hurry, they have a ready-made file of possibilities.

Helpful Hints

The official workday in most New York publishing offices begins at 9 A.M. and ends at 5 P.M. But most editors put in at least twelve-hour days during the work week, plus significant time on the weekends. They don't make a lot of money for their standard work week, and rarely, if ever, do they get overtime pay.

What to Expect of Your Editor

Somewhere among all those meetings, messages, and mounds of material, an editor has to find time to actually edit, too. And here's where writers' dreamy expectations are likely to hit the cold wall of reality with a thud. The truth is, the publishing world does not revolve around writers. Publishing does not change according to writers' demands or ideas of what should make it into print. It doesn't alter its schedule for your convenience. As we've mentioned elsewhere, you are the supplier of raw material in a complex manufacturing business. If you can't or won't provide the right material on time, publishers will find other suppliers who can and will.

The Acquisition Process

Whether you're pursuing publication in a magazine or with a book publisher, chances are the editor does not have the final say on offering a contract. Magazine editors may have to pitch story ideas they like to their colleagues, who may have different views about whether a particular piece will fit in with the magazine's theme or mission. Book editors have even more of a sales job; they have to convince their fellow editors, plus the sales, marketing, and publicity departments, that a book project is good for the house.

The process at both types of publishers can take weeks, or even months. Especially with book publishers, the yes-or-no decision can be made on anything from the reaction of the sales and marketing departments to an analysis of the project's profitability. At magazines, even if editors really like an idea, it might not fit in well with what has been planned for the next few issues, so they could defer a decision until they have an opening for it.

Helpful Hints

Don't pester editors to speed up approval of your idea. They are just as likely to issue a rejection in response to such behavior, because they simply don't have time to deal with overly demanding, unknown writers. If you hope to succeed as a professional writer, patience will be one of the most important tools you can master.

Praise and Criticism

Occasionally, you might run across an editor who loves your work to death and just can't stop telling you how great it is. Most writers' experience is quite different, though. You are more likely to get a quick "Nice work," possibly accompanied by a "Thanks!" and probably sent via e-mail. If you're like a lot of writers, this will be profoundly unsatisfying, even though it's a positive response. Most writers crave detailed feedback on their work. You want to know what an editor liked, what he didn't like, what turn of phrase worked for him and which parts came across as dull and uninspired.

Unfortunately, most editors are just too busy to provide that kind of critique on every piece they deal with. "Nice work, thanks" may seem curt and superficial, but, in reality, it's a great compliment. It means the editor didn't have to do a lot of work to your copy, that you fulfilled the assignment, and that the editor is free to devote his attention to other things. Editors love writers who deliver that kind of work; don't mistake lack of time for lack of appreciation.

The same holds true for criticism. Editors often don't have time to sugarcoat their criticisms, and they sure don't have time to coddle their writers. Their job is to make the piece work for the market, and every criticism they offer is aimed at making the material better. They are not out to destroy your self-esteem or ruin your work. Handling criticism is tough. You have to be tough and flexible enough to see the editor's point of view.

Helpful Hints

Ask editors about their pet peeves, and most of them will cite, among other things, writers who are too attached to their material. Words are only words, after all, and if you fall in love with your own words, it can blind you to their defects. Respect your editor's opinion; she might be seeing something you've missed.

What Your Editor Expects from You

Every writer wants definitive, inside information about what editors want. It's simpler than you might think, because every editor wants the same thing: something terrific. They want something that will make their pulses quicken, their eyes shine, and their ganglions vibrate. How do you do that? By crafting material with these qualities:

- Talent combined with a strong grasp of mechanics. Good grammar, syntax, punctuation, spelling—all count.
- Information-gathering skills. Provide accurate information in language readers will understand.
- Clear, concise, unpretentious writing. Inject your own style, but stay within the parameters of the editor's needs.
- Details that illustrate and illuminate your topic.
- An angle the editor hasn't thought of, presented in a way she hasn't thought of.

Editors keep reading the submission pile because of the high they get when they find what they're looking for. Combine terrific material with a professional attitude, and you just may be the answer to an editor's prayer.

Act Like a Professional

In publishing, "professional" means more than getting paid for what you do. It is as much about the way you comport yourself in your dealings with other pros. Understand the demands on an editor's time and energy and be respectful of those other demands when you need to claim the editor's attention. Don't call or e-mail without a good and compelling reason and remember that hounding him about your submission doesn't count as a good reason. Accept suggestions and criticisms with courtesy; fight for what's important, but choose your battles with care. Always be civil, even when you disagree.

Follow the Editor's Rules

Submission guidelines are developed to cope efficiently with the enormous volume of material editors receive. Think about the math involved here. The average magazine editor receives 1,500 or more submissions a year. That's 125 a month, nearly thirty a week, or about six every day. And you thought you got a lot of junk mail.

Helpful Hints

Novice writers sometimes think they can make themselves stand out from the crowd by ignoring the submission guidelines. Even if that's true, standing out doesn't necessarily improve your chances of getting published. All you really call attention to is the fact that you can't or won't follow directions—a red flag for the editors who might work with you.

Perhaps the worst thing about all those submissions, from an editor's standpoint, is that so many of them will be utterly wrong for him. Chances are that even the ones that are right for him will be irritants, because they'll come in a form he doesn't want, and no writer wants an irritated editor reading her stuff. If the editor prefers a query, send a query. If he doesn't want e-mail submissions, don't send him e-mail submissions. Experienced editors can tell within a few sentences whether a piece is right for them; it's a waste of your time and theirs to give them more than they need to make an informed judgment.

Search for the Right Fit

Part of being professional is matching your material to the right markets. Editors lose a lot of precious time dealing with submissions that aren't appropriate for them, and they are inclined to jump with incredulous joy when they find a submission that is perfectly tailored for their target readers. Study the market listings to find out who those target readers are and refine your material to fit the needs of those readers.

There's another element to finding the right fit: approaching the right editor. At magazines, the managing editor, executive editor, or editor-in-chief isn't necessarily the best person to address your query to. Check the masthead to find out which editors are in charge of which departments, like health and fitness, relationships, food, and so on. If your idea falls within one of those categories, send it to the editor responsible for it.

Likewise, editors at book publishers usually are responsible for specific imprints, series, or categories of books. Don't expect that the wrong editor will pass your material along to the right one. Take the time to find out who the correct recipient is before you drop anything in the mailbox.

Keep in mind that the information in market directories is invaluable, but it isn't infallible. Editors move to other jobs or to new responsibilities within their company. For magazines, pick up a current copy and check the masthead. For book publishers, check out the Web site or call the general phone number and ask if the editor you've targeted is still in charge of the line you want to query.

Solving Problems Together

In a perfect world, writers would submit spotless, complete copy well before deadline with facts triple-checked, so that all an editor would have to do is pass it along to the next person on the assembly line. In the world we live in, though, this is nothing more than a fantasy. Problems are bound to crop up in a business as complex as publishing. How you work with your editor to resolve those problems can mean the difference between minor aggravation and major headaches.

Respect Deadlines

Editors expect you to deliver what you promise when you promise to have it done. If something comes up that will prevent you from meeting your deadline, contact your editor immediately and explain the problem. (If you're working on a book manuscript and you have an agent, let the agent know about the problem. She can, and should, deal with the editor on your behalf.) Whenever possible, offer a solution to the problem. The main concern for an editor is getting the material she needs when she needs it. In many cases, she'll be willing to do what can be done.

Be Honest

Editors can't afford to work with writers who lie, plagiarize, or otherwise mislead them. Your behavior and performance reflect on your editor. Do good work, and it helps both of you; do poorly, and it hurts both of you. You have to supply original work. If you're writing nonfiction books or articles, you can't make up quotes or describe scenes that you haven't witnessed. When you supply your credentials, you can't lie about your background, experience, or previous credits. When you propose an idea, fiction or nonfiction, your material has to live up to what you promised.

Helpful Hints

To ensure your reputation doesn't suffer, don't make a habit of making mistakes. Promises to do better next time lose their luster when repeated too often, and even if you're as fast as a jackrabbit in repairing the damage, the smell of unreliability can linger over your name and your work.

Now, everyone knows that mistakes happen, and no one expects you to be perfect. If you make a mistake—attribute a quote to the wrong source, unintentionally lift a phrase or passage from a copyrighted work, or otherwise err—face up to it immediately and work with your editor to correct it as quickly and painlessly as possible. No matter how embarrassed or awkward you may feel, it's your responsibility to identify the problem and fix it. Editors can forgive a lot when their writers are responsive and responsible.

Beyond This Project

The key to establishing yourself as a professional writer is building relationships with editors. Burn an editor once, and you probably won't get another assignment from him; he might even warn his colleagues about you. But, if you come through for him on one piece, he's more likely to consider you for other assignments. And when you've built a good relationship with an editor, that will go with him to his next job.

It isn't difficult to establish a good relationship with an editor. Most of it is common sense and professional courtesy. Submit your copy on time and cover the subject you agreed to cover. Make sure your pieces are at least in the ballpark of the promised length. Give your editor the format she asked for. Understand what she needs for readers and tailor your pitches appropriately. Strive to resolve problems and differences of opinion quickly and amicably. Don't be disrespectful to her, her colleagues, or other writers.

Finally, give editors what they want: something wonderful. Excite them. Show them why your idea is important—not to you, but to their readers. Give them a fresh slant. Be a stickler for accuracy. Wrap it all up in writing that is clear, engaging, witty, stylish, and compelling. If you can do that and do it regularly, you'll have a professional ally for life, and you'll be well on your way to a rewarding career as a published writer.

Chapter 11

Make Your Book Known

Working with Others

Building buzz almost always begins inside the publishing house with your editor. She has almost as much at stake with your book as you do, especially if you're a first-time author, because, if your book does well, she'll look good to her bosses for recognizing your talent and the money-making potential of your book. She's the one who championed your idea to the pub board; her enthusiasm for your project inspired her colleagues. She'll talk up you and your book to the sales staff, who will talk up you and your book to the booksellers, who, in turn, just might talk up you and your book to their customers. However, important as such enthusiasm is, it goes only so far. The rest, almost always, will be up to you.

Helpful Hints

There are some books that do unexpectedly well and make lots of money for the publisher and the author. In the industry, these are called "break-out" books, and they achieve high sales figures despite a lack of marketing support from the publisher.

Reasonable Expectations

Spend any appreciable time with published writers, either in person or in online chat rooms, and eventually you'll come across a common complaint: Publishers don't spend enough time or money on promoting books. Many authors, disappointed by lackluster sales of their books, tend to blame their publishers; they believe their books would have soared to the top of the bestseller lists if only the publisher had invested more in marketing. But the hard truth is that almost every book published these days is going to appear in the bookstores without a major publicity campaign. They are simply too expensive for publishers to conduct, unless the book is already expected to be a bestseller.

If you expect your publisher to have you scheduled to appear on the *Today* show and *Good Morning America* the day your book hits the stores, or if you walk into your local bookstore expecting to see a giant poster of the cover of your book atop a table filled with dozens of copies right by the entrance, chances are you're going to be bitterly disappointed. The producers at the major networks aren't interested in interviewing new authors unless there's a news or celebrity angle to cover, and those displays at the front of your neighborhood Barnes & Noble or Borders store cost publishers tens of thousands of dollars. Such promotions are strictly reserved for commercial titles by, usually, authors who already have hit the bestseller lists with earlier books. They are extremely rare for new authors, most of whom are writing midlist books that may hit respectable sales figures but probably won't break out.

Promotion Realities

That said, there are things almost all publishers will do for almost all the books they put out. They usually send out press releases and review copies of their books to major newspapers around the country. They usually promote new titles prominently in their catalogs and on their Web sites. And they usually will coordinate media interviews when the media requests them.

Before you get too excited about even this modest marketing support, remember that it is extremely rare to get a review in a major newspaper, and small- and medium-sized newspapers often don't even have book reviewers on staff (and publishers usually won't send releases or review copies to these smaller markets, anyway). It's nice to have a full page devoted to your book in the publisher's catalog, but remember that those catalogs (and Web sites) are geared mainly toward booksellers, not to the general reading public. Finally, although the publicity department at your publishing house will handle requests for media interviews, the media isn't likely to be pestering them for an interview with an unknown author of an unknown book. These resources from the publisher are merely the first baby steps in getting your book in front of potential readers.

Helpful Hints

Only amateurs demand extravagant marketing support from their publishers. If your book is expected to become a huge commercial success, your publisher may schedule book tours and interviews with the national media. Otherwise, you'll get the same marketing support all other books get—i.e., a press release and a review copy sent to major media, and not much else.

What You Can Do

As you can see, chances are the bulk of the marketing work for your book will fall on your shoulders, at least until you do become famous (which, for many authors, doesn't happen until the third, fourth, or fifth book, if it happens at all). So, before you begin shopping your proposal or manuscript to an agent or editor, you'll need to think about what you can do to help promote your book. After all, no one else is going to care as much about your book's success as you do. That's the bad news. The good news is that you have more resources at your disposal than you think, no matter where you live and no matter what you write.

Issue Your Own Release

Your publisher likely will send out a general news release about your book, along with a review copy, to a few dozen major newspapers around the country. But this doesn't preclude you from sending out your own release, as long as you coordinate your efforts with your publisher's publicity department. You have a distinct advantage in doing this, because you can target your own local and regional media, using the same research skills you use in figuring out how to tailor your writing to specific markets.

When you're dealing with local media, your hook most likely will be the fact that you're a resident of your community rather than the topic or slant of your book. Everybody likes hometown bragging rights, whether it's the title-winning high school basketball team or having a bona fide author in their midst. Start with the newspapers, television stations, and radio stations that serve your geographic area, and clearly point out that you live in their service areas. Make sure your news release includes the following:

- Your name
- Your city, town, or village
- At least one phone number where you can be reached
- The title of your book
- The name of your publisher and the publication date
- A short paragraph describing your book
- A short bio on you

Keep your release to one page. Think of it as a query letter, only in this case you want to catch the attention of a reporter or an assignment editor. You have to convince him that this is a story worth pursuing and give him the means to pursue it—that is, your contact information and, if applicable, a Web site where he can find out more about you or your book.

Talk to Your Local Bookseller

Even the big chain booksellers have local or regional managers who arrange book signings and readings for local authors. Go to your neighborhood bookstore and introduce yourself as the author of your book, and ask for the name and phone number of the person who coordinates these things. Find out what the bookstore will do to promote a signing or reading, such as in-store posters, invitation lists, and press releases about the event. If the store personnel don't usually write press releases, ask if it's all right for you to issue one to local media. Even a small blurb in the "Community Calendar" section of your local newspaper helps spread the word about your book.

Schedule Local Appearances

Many civic, social, and religious organizations regularly schedule guest speakers for their meetings. Get in touch with the YMCA or YWCA, the Rotary or Kiwanis Club, and similar groups and offer to make a short presentation to their members. Reading circles and community book clubs, which seem to be regaining popularity in some areas of the country, also present good opportunities for you; many of them would jump at the chance to read your book and bring you in to discuss it with the group.

Always let an agent or editor know that you are available for book signings, media interviews, and other personal appearances, but expect to schedule these yourself, and expect to do it mainly on a local or regional level. This is where you'll be most effective, anyway, and it will be good practice for your eventual rise to a national stage.

Take Baby Steps

New authors—and even some seasoned professionals—commonly dream of sitting on a stage chatting with Oprah and her audience, discussing their books with Matt Lauer, or exchanging ideas with the amiable host of *Larry King Live*. There's nothing wrong with those dreams, but don't expect them to come true right away. There's a definite value in starting out small and building up to a national audience, both for creating sustainable buzz and for your own self-confidence.

Local Media

Your community newspaper is the perfect place to start your own public relations campaign. Many weeklies and even smaller dailies will print, word for word, a simple news release announcing the publication of your book. Larger newspapers probably won't print your release verbatim, but they might be interested in doing a profile on you as an interesting person in the community. If nothing else, you might end up with a paragraph about your book in the paper, and that, too, helps spread the word.

Helpful Hints

Press releases aren't always the most effective way to reach the media, especially your local newspaper or broadcast station. You might have better luck if you call the person responsible for book news with a quick pitch about your own book, and ask if he or she is interested in seeing a press release or review copy.

Check out local radio and television stations as well. Many news and talk radio stations have local programming where they profile local residents, and you might be a perfect guest for one of the shows. Likewise, many television stations have locally produced talk shows or segments on some of their newscasts devoted to people and events in the service area.

Depending on what your book covers, you also might be able to interest local or regional specialty publications in your book. If you've written a financial planning guide for college students, for example, the local business magazine might want to profile you and your book. The local entertainment weekly might be interested in your novel.

Go Back to School

Contact the English and journalism teachers in your area school districts and offer to speak to their classes about writing, the writing life, and becoming an author. Prepare a very brief presentation about yourself, no more than five minutes, and open the floor for questions. In case the students are shy, have questions ready to ask them; this will help break the ice. In nearly every class, there are at least one or two students who are passionate about writing and envision becoming writers themselves someday, and they will be eager, as every burgeoning writer is, to learn what you can teach them from your own experience. Just as important, these students (and their teachers) likely will talk about your presentation to parents, friends, and colleagues, which helps spread the word about you and your book.

Get Wired

Did you know that reporters routinely read blogs to find story ideas and sources for stories? A 2005 study sponsored by Columbia University reported that 53 percent of journalists use blogs to find story ideas, and 36 percent use them to find sources for stories. This is a great new promotion opportunity for authors, and you should be prepared to take advantage of it. Search the Internet for blogs that cover topics related to your book, then contact the host. You might be able to do a stint as a guest blogger on the site, or the host might even be interested in receiving a review copy of your book. Either way, it's another venue for you to spread the word about your book.

Helpful Hints

As blogs have become more popular, blog directories are cropping up all over the Internet. Use sites like Blogwise (*www.blogwise.com*) and Globe of Blogs (*www.globeofblogs.com*) to search for blogs by topic, geographic region, or author and find out how to get involved to promote your book or your own blog.

So how does this connect with reporters reading blogs? Most reporters have a stock list of experts they go to when they need a quote or other information for a story. At the same time, most of them are always on the lookout for new experts to turn to. Especially for nonfiction writers, having your name and your book on the appropriate blogs can quickly earn you entry into the source files of journalists all over the country, and even around the world.

Take Advantage of Your Platform

Whether you teach, lead conferences and seminars, or do stand-alone speaking engagements, you can turn virtually any personal appearance into a promotion opportunity. If your book is related to the courses you teach, you might be able to use it as a supplemental textbook for the class, or include it on your reading list. You can make copies of your book available to the people who attend your conferences and seminars, either by including it in the registration fee or by setting up a display and sales table at the back of the room. For speaking engagements, update your bio to include the title of your book, so the person who introduces you can inform your audience that you're the author.

Virtual Appearances

If you have a Web site or blog, be sure to update your site to include information about your book. Ideally, you should be able to show the book's cover, along with links to the publisher's Web site and to an online bookseller like Amazon.com or BarnesandNoble.com. And, of course, make sure your Web site includes a way to contact you.

You also might want to consider setting up an RSS (for Really Simple Syndication) feed from your site; this technology allows you to send periodic updates to people who subscribe (for free) to receive such information via e-mail. You can use an RSS feed to let people know what others are saying about your book, when you reach sales milestones, or even other news about you that might not be directly related to your book.

According to Nielsen/Net Ratings, *www.amazon.com* is routinely the second most popular multicategory commerce site on the Internet. It averages nearly 8 million unique visitors a week, each of whom spends an average of just over twelve minutes browsing the site. A link from your site to *www.amazon.com* is an easy way to direct potential sales of your book.

Tout Your Expertise

Once you've written and published a book (particularly nonfiction), you are considered an expert on the topic. Published novelists can be considered experts, too, on their genre and on creative writing in general. However, you probably will have to seek out opportunities to show off your expertise. Start by using search engines to find recent news stories on your topic and contact information for the reporter who wrote the story; many newspapers today include reporters' phone numbers and e-mail addresses at the end of their stories.

Helpful Hints

Reporters get a lot of spam e-mail, including e-mailed news releases. To bypass spam filters and junk e-mail folders, be as specific as you can in the subject line of your e-mail. Precise subject lines such as "Re: Your June 22 article on fad diets" or "Tips for your 'Cooking Healthy' column" are more likely to be opened and read.

When you find appropriate articles and contacts, send a brief e-mail to the reporter saying that you read his story and enjoyed it. Then tell him that the next time he needs information on that topic, you are available for interviews. You can point out (after you've said you enjoyed his article) an angle that his story didn't cover, interesting facts and figures, and the like. Be sure to do this tactfully; you won't make any friends if you come across as accusatory or arrogant. Finally, be sure to include your contact information so he can get in touch with you for future articles.

You can do the same thing with radio and television journalists. Again, the best way to do this usually is by e-mail, because it's less intrusive than a phone call and gives the reporter a written record for his files. If you decide to call, be sure to ask if the reporter has a few minutes; he may be working on deadline, which means he won't have time to chat.

Network, Network, Network

First-time authors usually have little trouble disposing of their free author's copies. They're so proud and excited to see the fruits of their labors that they hand out autographed copies to every relation and friend they can think of, and the relations and friends gladly accept them, even if they aren't interested in actually reading the book. But this is only the first step in accessing your network.

If you're like most people, your network probably is bigger than you think. It consists of the people you know, and of the people they know as well. The challenge for you is figuring out how to spread the word through the people you know, who will spread it to the people they know, and so on. One way to do this is to always keep business cards handy. Make sure they include your name, e-mail address, Web site, and the name of your book; if you want to get fancy, you can even put an image of your book's cover on one side of the card. Give them to business contacts, friends, and relatives, and give them permission to pass them along to their own circle of contacts.

If you belong to a church or civic group, find out if you can put an announcement in the group's newsletter about your book. If you have a day job (other than your own writing), see if the employee newsletter would be interested in doing a short piece on you and your book. If your neighborhood grocery store has a community bulletin board, ask the manager if it's okay to put up a small poster announcing the publication of your book. (Be sure to include on such a poster that you're a resident of the community—bragging rights count here, too.)

Helpful Hints

Some authors, especially self-published ones, try to market their books by buying promotional items like pens, bookmarks, mouse pads, and magnets emblazoned with their name, Web site, or the name of their book. But your best weapon isn't advertising. Save your money and concentrate your efforts on publicity, which is both effective and free.

Because writing is a solitary activity, many writers feel shy and uncomfortable talking about their books or other publishing successes. Sometimes even fielding compliments can feel uncomfortable. But remember that getting published still is enough of a rarity that most people are genuinely impressed by it, and they genuinely enjoy meeting a bona fide author. It's okay to take pride in your work and to let other people know about it, and it's okay to enjoy the warm glow you get when people praise your ability and congratulate you on your success.

Parlaying Coverage

When it comes to marketing, parlaying coverage means doing the work once and getting two or more pieces of publicity out of it. Businesses do this all the time. When a car dealer gets an award for its service department, or when a hotel is rated four diamonds by AAA, you'll probably see both a news story about the award or rating and then you'll see it in the business' advertising.

You can do the same thing in marketing your writing. If you're getting an award for something, even if it isn't related to your writing, send a news release to your local newspaper announcing it, and be sure to note that you're the author of your book. It doesn't have to be lengthy or complicated. It can be as simple as this:

> *Jim Robinson of West Suburb will receive the Volunteer of the Year award from the Greater Metropolis Chamber of Commerce at the annual meeting May 18. Robinson, who founded the Greater Metropolis Literacy Project, also is the author of* The Great American Novel *(Big City Publishers, September 2005).*

As always, be sure to include your contact information. You never know when a small thing like this might lead to bigger things. Even a small blurb in the local media puts your name (and the title of your book) in the public eye, and there's a possibility that the editors of the local media will think there's a good story in a profile of you, which further promotes you and your book. Think of parlaying coverage as connecting the dots for the folks in the media. They might not be interested in your award alone, and they may not be interested solely in the fact that you've had a book published. But, by putting the two together, you increase the news value of even the shortest blurb, thus improving your chances of getting the coverage you want.

Be Aware of Opportunities

Participating in activities that aren't directly related to your writing or your book can nevertheless help promote both, and doing so also helps your efforts to parlay coverage. One author agreed to do a book signing as part of a fundraiser for her local library. She donated her free author's copies of two of her books for the event and wrote a news release for the local newspaper. The hook for the news release was the fundraiser, but the news release also pointed out that the author was a local resident. That led to a profile of the author in the local newspaper, which mentioned all of the author's books, including an upcoming one.

Helpful Hints

Nearly all newspapers subscribe to wire services like the Associated Press, and these services are always looking for timeless features that are of interest to other member papers. If you live in Iowa, a profile of you in the *Fort Dodge Messenger* could easily get picked up by AP and run in several other Iowa newspapers.

If people in your community are talking about you and your book, word will get to the people in the next community, who will pass it on to the community further down the road. Do what you can to get that initial splash, regardless of size, and the ripples will take care of themselves.

Chapter 12

"I'm a Writer Now"

Great Expectations

Many writers believe they could be the next Hemingway if they could just escape the daily grind most of the world is accustomed to and spend all their time and energy on writing. Words would flow like honey, thick and rich, and there would be no such things as pressure or writer's block. Life would be one grand sweet song if all they had to do all day was write.

Sounds great in theory. In practice, it's an altogether different song. Even the people who don't have other jobs to pay the bills don't spend their days doing nothing but writing. They do the same things all other writers have to do—coming up with ideas, checking the markets, keeping files and records straight, negotiating contracts, coping with deadlines, and, occasionally, battling writer's block. When you make the jump from working for a paycheck to writing full-time, you don't just become a writer. You also become a salesperson, an office manager, a bill collector, a financial analyst, a business planner, a researcher, and your very own crisis counselor. And you do all that without any guarantee of a steady paycheck, or indeed of any kind of pay.

Helpful Hints

Writing is a solitary activity, but writers should get out in the world on a regular basis. Real-life experience, even through a part-time job or volunteer work, enriches your writing and keeps it in perspective. The best writing isn't done in a self-imposed vacuum; it incorporates the color, texture, and feelings of life in all its variety and complexity.

This isn't meant to discourage you from pursuing your dream. It's a reality check, so you know what you're getting into when you decide to go for it. Trying to squeeze in quality writing time around all your other commitments is tough, but being disillusioned and disappointed by your dreams is worse. If you're well-informed and well-prepared for what lies ahead, the unique challenges of becoming a full-time, self-employed writer won't seem quite as daunting.

Preparing the Ground

Financial planners always advise us to save between three and six months' worth of household expenses to avoid calamity in the event of a job loss. That's also what you should plan to have in the bank if you're planning to quit your regular job to write full-time. You'll be losing a steady income, and unless you already have contracts in place for articles, short stories, or books, chances are you won't see any money from your writing for quite a long time. Remember, query to response can take two to six weeks; completing the assignment can take another two weeks to several months; acceptance of the work and authorization of payment can take another one to three months; and, if you don't get paid until publication, it'll be several more months before you see any money. That's a long time to go without groceries or gas money.

One way to prepare for this is to save all the money you can so you have a comfortable amount to live on while your career ramps up. If you're in a domestic partnership or marriage, look for ways to cut expenses so you can live comfortably on one income, and put your paycheck in the savings account until you make the switch. This will give you a larger cushion for emergencies and other unplanned expenses until you begin to receive income from your writing.

Also plan for the loss of benefits, if you have them, when you quit your job. How will you pay for health insurance, for example? Vacations? Retirement savings? Many of us take these things for granted because they're provided by our employers. Once you're on your own, though, you'll be responsible for paying and planning for all these things. Gone will be automatic deductions for such things as 401(k) plans and Christmas clubs, and if you get sick or decide to take a week off to visit your sister in Wyoming, no one will be paying you for the time you spend not working.

Setting Goals

When you set out to write full-time, you're taking responsibility for managing your time and following your vision. To do that effectively, set specific goals for yourself, both short-term and long-term. If your ultimate goal is to become a book author, but you don't have the right platform or credentials to support that effort right now, then your short-term goals should be to build that platform and collect those credentials. Don't be afraid of starting small and building from there; that's the way most careers are made, and not just in publishing. Besides, each small step you take brings you that much closer to your big dream, and it's easier to keep yourself motivated if you can measure your progress rather than focus on how distant your dream still seems.

Make your short-term goals ones that are within your control. A goal of getting published in *GQ* is laudable, but you can't force that to happen. A more realistic goal would be to submit appropriate material to, say, six national magazines. That opens up many more possibilities for you, even if *GQ* isn't the right market for your work.

Making a Schedule

When you're completely on your own, it's easy to fritter your time away in daydreams, household chores, anything but writing and writing-related tasks. Like all self-employed people, successful full-time writers are self-starters, able to set a schedule for their work and stick to it, at least most of the time. They usually have a plan for the day, and maybe even a self-imposed quota for the work they want to get done. They take their self-employment as seriously as any traditional job, knowing that if they don't dedicate their time and energy to what needs to be done, no one else is there to do it for them.

Helpful Hints

Time has a remarkable illusory quality, which is what makes it slip away so quickly even when we think we have plenty of it. Goals, schedules, and self-imposed deadlines keep time from escaping you and turn it into the valuable tool it is for your writing career.

You can arrange your schedule any way you like; that's part of the freedom of being self-employed. You might prefer to write in the mornings and reserve your afternoons for attending to queries, submissions, and market research; you might prefer to reverse that. You might not feel the need to divide your time that way, instead deciding to be seated at your desk by nine o'clock each morning and prioritizing that day's tasks. Whatever works for you is fine. Just make sure you don't putter along for three months and suddenly discover that you haven't completed a project or sent out a query.

Creating a Business Plan

Once you've decided to become a full-time writer, you've also decided to become a small business owner. And, like any other small business owner, you'll need to have a plan for the success of your enterprise. Setting goals and a schedule will help you do that. But you also have to think like a business person.

Income and Expenses

Always keep copies of checks and receipts. You can use the check copies to check your year-end earnings statements from publishers, and receipts will help you track the expenses associated with your writing. You also should have an expense diary, where you can record the amount and other details of an expense when you don't have a receipt.

If you earn $600 or more from a single publisher, you'll receive IRS Form 1099 at the end of the year, which will state all your earnings from that particular publisher. The $600 threshold is an IRS requirement, but some publishers send out 1099s for earnings of less than $600, too. If you sell your work to more than one publisher during a calendar year, you should receive a 1099 from each of them.

Helpful Hints

If you have an agent, he or she will send you a 1099 listing all your earnings that passed through the agent's office. This usually will not include magazine sales, because most agents don't handle such sales. Your 1099 from your agent should reflect only the monies you actually received, not including the agent's commission.

On the expense side, you need to keep track of such things as office supplies, equipment (computers, copiers, fax machines, etc.), postage and shipping costs, book purchases and magazine subscriptions (related to your writing), membership dues to writers' organizations, conference expenses, and travel expenses, including taxi fares, tolls, parking fees, and mileage. As long as these expenses are related to your writing, you can claim them as deductions on your income tax return. If you aren't sure whether an expense is a valid deduction, keep a record of it and ask your tax preparer about it at tax time.

Writing-related deductions, including deductions for a home office, are generally limited to your writing income in any given year. If your expenses exceed your income, you can't deduct the extra expenses, but you might be able to carry them over into the next year, as long as your writing doesn't fall under the IRS "hobby rule." To avoid that, do your best to show a profit from your writing in at least three out of five years.

Business Structures

Most writers, at least at the beginning of their careers, don't bother with setting up a formal business structure. Even when you're self-employed as a writer and have no other job-related income, your writing business is considered a sole proprietorship—the simplest and most basic business structure. As a sole proprietor, you don't have to file separate business income tax returns; you can attach Schedule C to your personal income tax form.

As your career progresses, however, you might want to consider a more formal business arrangement. You can set up a limited liability company, or LLC; bestselling authors sometimes set up separate LLCs for each of their books, which can protect other assets in the event of a lawsuit. Other options include partnerships (you and at least one other person) and corporations. Each state has its own laws regarding each of these structures, and there are pros and cons to each. Do some research and consult an attorney before deciding whether it makes sense for you to go beyond the sole proprietorship structure.

Accessing Markets

Whether you're writing part-time or full-time, a good share of your time and energy will go into researching markets. Many beginning writers make the mistake of placing imaginary limits on what they can write and what they want to write. But, when you've made the full-time commitment to writing, you'll benefit from expanding your horizons when it comes to searching for places to sell your work.

Helpful Hints

Local governments sometimes hire freelance writers to help them apply for grants or get the word out on upcoming special elections or issues affecting residents. Professional grant writers usually charge a flat fee, plus a small percentage of the awarded grant, for their services. Other projects can be written for a flat fee or on an hourly basis, usually with a not-to-exceed maximum.

Try putting your various writing projects into one of two categories: the personal project, and the business project. The personal project is the one that speaks to your writer's soul, the one you can't wait to work on, the one that makes you want to be a writer in the first place. The business project is one that will further your writing career by giving you another clip for your portfolio and, one hopes, a boost to your bank balance. Business projects also can be used to bring you closer to your long-term goals. If you want to write a book for middle-school children about scuba diving, you should try to sell articles on similar topics to magazines aimed at younger readers.

Fiction writers in particular should remain open to nonfiction writing opportunities. In book publishing, it's easier for new writers to break in with a nonfiction book than with a novel, and a nonfiction book credit will help convince an agent or editor that you're capable of writing book-length work. The competition in magazine markets also is stiffer for fiction than for nonfiction, so you might find it easier to break in there, too. You can still relate your nonfiction to your fiction; magazine credits on scuba diving, marine life, and related topics add credibility to your pitch for that middle-school adventure novel set aboard a modern-day cruise ship.

Juggling Projects and Deadlines

One of the biggest challenges facing full-time writers is managing time. When you don't have a regular day job, it's easy to fool yourself into thinking you have plenty of time to do lots of writing projects; you tend to forget about other obligations of daily life, like running to the grocery store, doing the laundry, attending your children's soccer games or concerts or plays, and spending time with your family and friends. Because your schedule is your own as a full-time writer, it's your responsibility to be realistic about what you can and cannot do.

Keep Track of Your Projects

One of your first priorities should be to devise a system for keeping track of your projects. Professional writers usually have several projects going at once, in various stages of development. They may be working against a deadline for a magazine article on fly fishing, researching another article on the history of jousting, polishing a short story for submission, and working on plot points for a novel, all while waiting for responses to a query about a nonfiction book on herbal medicine.

Helpful Hints

Calendars make convenient tracking devices; you can note when you mailed your material, when you should expect a response, when your deadlines are, and professional and personal events. Having all this data in one place also can help you plan your schedule and determine whether you have enough time to do additional projects.

Even if you're not quite that busy yet, you need a way to keep tabs on the details of each of your projects. There's no right or wrong way to create a system that works and is convenient for you. It should include such things as what you submitted (a query, a completed article, a proposal, etc.), where you submitted it, when you should expect to get a response (based on listings in the market directories), and where you plan to send it next if this market doesn't pick it up.

Your tracking system also should include a to-do list for projects that aren't ready to be marketed yet and an organized filing system to keep the details of each project together. If each of your projects has its own file folder, you can keep all the paperwork associated with that project, such as rejection slips or e-mails, in that folder, and that lets you see at a glance the history and progress of that particular project. Given that months can go by between when you submit something and when you receive a response, such a filing system helps refresh your memory. It also gives you a place to put notes about new developments or ideas relating to that project.

Stagger Deadlines

A common mistake among new writers is bunching up project deadlines. It is possible, and sometimes even desirable, to work on more than one project at a time, but it's also extraordinarily easy to stretch yourself too thin. And, when that happens, chances are you won't be doing your best work on any of your current projects.

Sometimes writers are afraid to say no to assignments, even when the deadlines conflict with prior obligations. Your natural instinct, especially when you're just starting out to live your dream, is to grab every opportunity that comes your way, even if it means that you won't have time to sleep for the next six weeks. But you aren't always stuck in the take-it-or-leave-it trap when it comes to deadlines. If you think you'll have difficulty meeting a deadline, for any reason—other projects, a scheduled vacation, or whatever—ask the agent or editor if the deadline is negotiable. You might be surprised at how willing editors and publishers are to adjust schedules for projects and writers they really want.

There are advantages to working on more than one project at a time. Having several projects in the hopper helps ease the natural worries most writers have about receiving rejections. When you always have another idea to be polished and fitted for the right market, you're less likely to obsess about the fate of one of your other ideas.

Protecting Your Reputation

Perhaps more than any other business, success in publishing depends as much on your professional image and reputation as it does on your talent and ideas. These intangible qualities can influence your career in ways you may never even realize. Editors who have had good experiences with you, or who have heard about what a treat you are to work with, often will seek you out when they have assignments that you're well-suited for. Such instances mean much more than just a warm and fuzzy feeling for your ego; they mean less work for you in market research and querying, because the projects are coming to you. So your reputation is an asset worth investing in and protecting.

Follow Business Etiquette

You project an image in your first contact with an agent or editor, and that image will color, for good or bad, the project you're hoping to sell. This is why following the submission guidelines is important. They aren't designed to exclude you from publishing's paradise. They are designed to separate the desirable grain from the undesirable chaff in the most efficient way possible. Sidestepping or ignoring the guidelines more than likely will flag your material as chaff. Following the guidelines improves your odds of being picked up as grain. Take these steps to establish and protect your reputation on paper:

- Get the name and publication or company of the recipient right, and use courtesy titles (Mr., Ms.) until you're invited to use first names. If you don't know whether the recipient is a man or woman, use the full name in addresses and salutations.
- Make sure your name, address, telephone number (with area code), and e-mail address appears on every piece of correspondence with an agent or editor.
- Double-check your SASEs to make sure they include the proper postage and your own address.
- Use standard business and manuscript formatting—single-spaced for query and cover letters, double-spaced for manuscript pages, with at least one-inch margins all around.
- Print all submissions only on one side of the page. Never handwrite submissions.
- Send all submission materials in one package—cover letter, SASE, sample chapters or completed pieces, etc.

Business etiquette applies to telephone manners, too. Once you get an assignment or build a relationship with an agent or editor, some of your communication will be done over the phone. It's important to remember that this is still a business communication, and you should strive to be on your best professional behavior. Some tips for achieving that:

- Keep your mouth free of gum, pens, food, and other foreign objects when you're on the phone.
- Use your normal speaking voice; don't whisper, and don't shout, even on a cell phone.
- Use professional language. Don't swear or use vulgar expressions.
- Avoid multi-tasking. Don't try to work on your computer, sort the mail, or wash the dishes while you're on the phone.
- Keep the conversation on track. Editors and agents rarely have time for idle chit-chat.
- Don't call unless it's absolutely necessary.
- When it is absolutely necessary to call, always ask first if this is a good time to talk. If it isn't, ask for a more convenient time, and, whenever possible, agree graciously to postpone the call until then.

The prevalence and convenience of e-mail has greatly reduced the amount of time authors have to spend on the phone with agents and editors. E-mail is an efficient and less intrusive method for exchanging information, asking and answering questions, and even scheduling phone dates. If you can't decide whether you should call or e-mail an agent or editor, always e-mail first; it's respectful of the agent's or editor's time, and usually you can get what you need.

Helpful Hints

Don't call agents or editors with queries, to press for a decision on a submission, to deliver progress updates, or to complain about a rejection. This wastes time and marks you as an amateur. Even when you're established and the rules for submitting ideas relax a little, e-mail and snail mail remain the preferred contact methods for most agents and editors.

Keeping Your Promises

Professional writers are honest in their dealings with agents and editors, and they don't make promises they can't keep. Whenever you submit a query or other material (even before you have a contract, which puts these promises in writing), you are making an implicit promise that you're telling the truth about yourself and your work. That means you don't claim to be a published author if you're not, you don't claim to have endorsements that you don't have, you don't try to pass off someone else's material as your own, and you don't agree to deadlines that you can't meet. Misleading an agent or editor puts a big black mark against your name and, potentially, your future as a writer.

That said, and this being an imperfect world, there may be times when you can't keep some of your promises for reasons that are beyond your control. Accidents, sudden illness, technical problems, and other unforeseen issues might interfere with your ability to meet a deadline, for example. When these things happen, communicate with your agent and editor. Don't make excuses, but do explain the problem and outline a plan for getting back on track. Facing the issue squarely and immediately is the hallmark of a true professional, and it is the only protection you have for your reputation when things don't go as planned.

It's important to always keep the lines of communication open with your agent or editor. Don't ignore e-mails and phone calls. If you don't have time to respond fully right away, at least send a message acknowledging the contact and stating when you'll be free to address it. Then be sure to live up to your promise of following up.

Cooperation

Most agents and editors prefer to see themselves as part of a team with their authors. The team's goal is to provide the best possible content for readers, with each member of the team contributing substantially to the overall success of the project. Unfortunately, too many authors dismiss this model and instead view agents and editors as obstructionist and recalcitrant, or even as enemies. Obviously, the reputation these authors earn isn't one of professionalism.

Rejections and criticism are integral parts of the publishing game. Learn to receive them with aplomb, at least publicly. If you feel the need to rant and rave, do it in private. Defend your point of view, but do it with a civil tongue and an effort to see the other's perspective.

Helpful Hints

One of the simplest ways to protect your reputation is to make sure you always have a backup of your work. Whether you print a hard copy, make a disk, or e-mail your work to yourself, routinely backing up everything you write is cheap insurance against technical catastrophes. You'll be awfully glad you have it when you need it.

The spirit of cooperation also comes into play when there are the inevitable glitches in the publishing process. Delays, questions, disagreements, and confusion are frustrating for everyone, but they don't always have to be crises. Train yourself to respond quickly and efficiently to such things, and to recognize and accept when the situation is beyond your ability to correct.

The old philosophy, "What goes around comes around," should be your guide here. The more patient, understanding, and cooperative you are when the problem is not your doing or your responsibility, the more likely you are to receive the same treatment when your circumstances require it.

Measuring Your Rewards

A great advantage to being self-employed, whether as a writer or in another profession, is that you get to define your own measures of success. You decide what is most important to you, what trade-offs you're willing to make, and what kind of balance you want. Most of us have several success yardsticks, but they usually can be divided into two broad categories: financial rewards and emotional rewards.

Go for the Money

As a full-time writer, the money will be important to you. You want to be able to support yourself, even if you never see the mega-bucks advances of celebrities and bestselling authors. If you're like most writers, you'll start out working for very small checks. As you gain more experience, the complexity and length of your assignments will rise, as will your per-word rate. You'll make your way into larger markets with a higher profile, which in turn will make you more salable to even bigger markets. Very likely, you'll get to a point where you have to turn down low-paying assignments so you have enough time to devote to the better-paying ones.

This is a natural progression, though it sometimes is a slow one. When you're a rookie, people in publishing will not value your talent or your time as highly. But, if you stick with it and do what's required to establish and maintain your credibility as a writer, the money will come.

Go for the Joy

Throughout this book, we've shown you how to approach writing as a business and a vocation. This is information you need if you want to fulfill your dreams of getting published and reap the rewards that go along with that accomplishment. But, even when it's work, writing should be fun. It should be stimulating and challenging. And that should be what motivates you to sit down and do the work.

But writing, like any other line of work, can grow stale, particularly if you lock yourself into a narrow niche and think you have to stay there for the rest of your career. It's true that writers, especially in fiction, and especially when just starting out, are expected to pick a genre and stick with it for at least their first two books; it helps build your readership and assists in marketing efforts to tap into and expand that base. But, even for novelists, there are ways around that, such as using different pen names for different genres.

Helpful Hints

The pay rates listed in the market directories aren't set in stone. As a new, unknown writer, you might be offered less than what is listed; as an established writer with a solid reputation for delivering good material on time, you can negotiate for more. Use the market listings as a ballpark estimate rather than a guarantee.

If you find that your writing career is losing its freshness, think about ways to recapture the joy of writing. This might mean keeping a personal project close at hand and taking periodic breaks from your business projects to work on your labor of love. It might mean taking the risks you had to take at the beginning of your career, stretching your skills and trying different styles and being willing to face rejection in a new format or market. It might even mean taking a break from writing altogether, until you feel the old, familiar itch in your fingertips that signals the formulation of a new and grand idea.

One of the terrific things about writing is that there's no mandatory retirement age. You have a whole lifetime to explore any kind of writing you like, and that's a fringe benefit you won't find in many other vocations. As a full-time writer, always be aware of where your joy is. Sometimes, it's the only thing that makes the trials and tribulations of the writing life truly worthwhile. If you lose track of it, don't be afraid to go looking for it again.

Appendix

Sample Query Letters and Proposals

The following pages contain sample query letters for both magazine articles and book ideas, as well as a sample nonfiction book proposal and cover letter and a sample fiction synopsis and query letter. You'll notice that the magazine query (page 164), which is for an essay rather than a feature article, doesn't talk about market, but it does talk about the magazine's readership. The nonfiction book query (page 165), on the other hand, does talk about the market, because part of the pitch is showing the agent or editor that there's a large potential readership for your book.

Meg Schneider
123 North Street
Suburbia NY 12345
(555) 222-2222
MegSchneider@myemailaddress.com

Joseph Brown, Editor
The Best Writing Magazine Ever
P.O. Box 1111
Middle America, KS 45678

April 27, 2005

Dear Mr. Brown,

I am *way* too normal to be a writer. Handicapped by a happy childhood, wise and loving parents, a fun and fulfilling marriage, and no worse addiction than an occasional intense craving for a proper Philly cheese steak, I am doomed to eternal exclusion from that elite class of unhappy souls known the world over as Great Writers.

Or so I have always been told.

It took me nearly two decades of earning my living as a writer to reach an epiphany that, unfortunately, escapes most aspiring writers: There is no rule requiring writers to suffer the tortures of the damned in order to be any good as writers.

To help your readers avoid torturing themselves about not being tortured enough, I have written an essay titled "Too Happy to be a Writer" for your "From the Desk of" department. It is 1,012 words.

I am an award-winning writer with 17 years' experience in television, radio, newspaper and public relations. My book credits include *Everything Writing a Book Proposal* (Adams Media, May 2005), *Everything Casino Gambling* (Adams Media, September 2004), and *The Birth Order Effect for Couples* (Fair Winds Press, January 2004). My contact information is listed above.

Thank you for your time and consideration. I look forward to hearing from you.

Sincerely,
Meg Schneider

Meg Schneider
123 North Street
Suburbia NY 12345
(555) 222-2222
MegSchneider@myemailaddress.com

K.C. Jones, President
Jones Literary Agency
333 E. Washington Street, Suite 201
Big Apple NY 01010

April 27, 2005

Dear K.C. Jones,

According to a study by the Hobby Industry Association, 60 percent of all U.S. households engaged in some kind of craft-making or hobby activity in the past year, and 77 percent of all households have at least one member who has engaged in craft-making. Retail craft and hobby stores represent a $29-billion-a-year business.

For the beginning crafter, the plethora of choices, and the expense of selecting the wrong medium, can be daunting. Painting, needlework, stamping and stenciling, sewing, furniture refinishing, scrapbooking—the menu is vast and intimidating, especially for those who don't know yet which medium is the right one for them.

THE BIG BOOK OF CRAFTING: EXPRESS YOUR CREATIVITY THROUGH EASY, INEXPENSIVE HOME CRAFTS solves that problem for would-be crafters. Designed specifically for beginners, THE BIG BOOK OF CRAFTING encourages readers to experiment with a variety of crafts before making a huge investment in equipment and supplies. Indeed, many of the tools and supplies listed in this book can be used for two or more different categories of crafts, adding further value for the reader.

I am a lifelong dabbler in a wide array of home crafts and an award-winning writer with 17 years' experience in television, radio, newspaper and public relations. My book credits include *Everything Writing a Book Proposal* (Adams Media, May 2005), *Everything Casino Gambling* (Adams Media, September 2004), and *The Birth Order Effect for Couples* (Fair Winds Press, January 2004). My contact information is listed above.

Thank you for your time and consideration. I look forward to hearing from you.

Sincerely,
Meg Schneider

Meg Schneider
123 North Street
Suburbia NY 12345
(555) 222-2222
MegSchneider@myemailaddress.com

K.C. Jones, President
Jones Literary Agency
333 E. Washington Street, Suite 201
Big Apple NY 01010

June 27, 2005

Dear K.C. Jones,

Enclosed is the proposal you requested for THE BIG BOOK OF CRAFTING:
EXPRESS YOUR CREATIVITY THROUGH EASY, INEXPENSIVE HOME
CRAFTS. It is envisioned as a one-stop shop for aspiring and beginning crafters
who want to experiment with different media before making a significant investment in supplies and equipment.

Although there are dozens of craft books on the market, I have been unable to find
a comprehensive guide aimed at adults who are just starting their foray into the
highly popular and ever-expanding world of home crafts.

Thank you for your interest and your time. I look forward to hearing from you.

Sincerely,
Meg Schneider

THE BIG BOOK OF CRAFTING:

Express Your Creativity Through Easy, Inexpensive Home Crafts

By

Meg Schneider
123 North Street
Suburbia NY 12345
(555) 222-2222
MegSchneider@myemailaddress.com

CONTENTS

OVERVIEW

THE BIG BOOK OF CRAFTING: EXPRESSING YOUR CRE-
ATIVITY THROUGH EASY, INEXPENSIVE HOME CRAFTS
is the essential beginner's portal into the fast-growing world of home
crafts. Whether your affinity is painting, stitching, stenciling, flower
arranging or furniture refinishing, THE BIG BOOK OF CRAFTING
shows you how to get started and takes you step-by-step through the
process from great idea to fabulous finished product.

THE BIG BOOK OF CRAFTING covers 20 of the most popular
home crafts, including scrapbooking, beading, home and holiday décor
and decorations, and all manner of stitch-and-sew crafts. Each chapter
includes a list of materials and suggestions on where to find them, key
tips like how to use a hot-glue gun and how to choose colors, and tricks
to make home crafting even easier and more enjoyable. Easy-to-follow
instructions are accompanied by photos and illustrations that show the
reader exactly how to complete each step. Along the way, readers also
will find inspiration for unleashing their own inner creativity.

THE BIG BOOK OF CRAFTING is the first comprehensive beginner's guide to home crafts. It is approximately 80,000 words.

ABOUT THE AUTHOR

Meg Schneider

Meg Schneider is an award-winning writer with more than a decade of experience in television, radio and print journalism, and an avid crafter of long standing. She is the co-author of "Birth Order for Couples" (Rockport Publishers, January 2004), author of "The Everything Casino Gambling Book" (Adams Media, 2004) and co-author of "The Everything Book Proposals Book" (Adams Media, 2005).

When Schneider isn't writing, she is painting, cross-stitching, stenciling, weaving, or refinishing some project destined for her own home, a friend's or relative's home, or the monthly craft fair down the road from her house. Through her community's Adult and Community Education program, she has taught more than a dozen classes on various crafting techniques to more than 300 students. She also has been invited to speak at craft and hobby conventions throughout the Northeast and has been profiled in *Ain't Crafting Grand* magazine.

Her journalism honors include awards from the Iowa Associated Press Managing Editors, Women in Communications, the Maryland-Delaware-D.C. Press Association, Gannett, the New York State Associated Press, and the William Randolph Hearst Foundation.

A native of Iowa, Schneider now lives in Upstate New York with her husband and three dogs.

THE MARKET

According to a study by the Hobby Industry Association, 60 percent of all U.S. households engaged in some kind of craft-making or hobby activity in 2002, and 77 percent of all households have at least one member who has, at some point, engaged in craft-making. Retail craft and hobby stores reported $29 billion in sales in 2002, a 13 percent increase over the previous year.

To reach these consumers, media groups have launched dozens of magazines, some targeted at a general crafting readership and some aimed more precisely at woodworkers, sewers, quilters, knitters, and so on. Three of the largest of the general craft magazines—*Michael's Create!, Creating Keepsakes,* and *Craft Magazine*—have a combined circulation of 750,000.

General home-and-lifestyle consumer magazines such as *Better Homes and Gardens, Family Circle, Good Housekeeping* and *Woman's Day* have added regular crafting features to their editorial line-ups. The top 10 magazines in this category have a combined circulation of approximately 37 million.

In addition to the plethora of craft shows on public and cable television, not to mention regular segments on national morning news programs such as "Today," major newspapers, including *The Wall Street Journal* and the *New York Times,* have reported extensively on the popularity of crafts and the success of craft businesses.

Craft and cooking books comprise the third-largest category of book sales in the U.S., and general nonfiction, including humor, is the fourth-largest category.

THE BIG BOOK OF CRAFTING could capture a respectable portion of the crafting market as a gift idea for the crafter in your home or an idea generator for crafters.

PROMOTION

Aside from the usual bookselling outlets, THE BIG BOOK OF CRAFTING has great potential in the gift market, particularly among crafters and their friends and relatives. It likely would do well in gift stores and other non-traditional retail locations.

CRAFTING's short, snappy prose lends itself to being excerpted in magazines and on web sites, such as MSNBC.com's "Today Show Book Club."

CRAFTING also can be promoted effectively through personal appearances by the author and her collection of homemade craft items. The author is available for book signings, media interviews and speaking engagements.

Various crafting organizations, such as the national Craft & Hobby Association, the Home Sewing Association, the National Needlework Association, and the Society of Craft Designers, also are excellent promotional vehicles.

CRAFTING also can be promoted on the Internet via the author's web site and links on scores of craft sites.

COMPETITION

While there are dozens of home craft books on the market, there is no single comprehensive craft book for adults that covers the full range of popular home crafts. THE BIG BOOK OF CRAFTING fills a void left by these other books by providing readers with essential information on all major crafts in one volume. This approach is particularly useful for beginners, who may want to experiment with many different kinds of crafts before they find the medium they most enjoy.

Because it covers the full range of home crafts, THE BIG BOOK OF CRAFTING can be compared with the Better Homes & Gardens series of crafting books, including 10 CRAFTS UNDER $10 (2003) and PAINTED CRAFTS (1990) as well as more specific books like CREATIVE FLORAL ARRANGING (Home Decorating Institute, 1997), NEW METAL FOIL CRAFTS (Rockport Publishers, 2002), and SEW SIMPLE SQUARES (Watson-Guptill Publications, 2003).

OUTLINE

The INTRODUCTION discusses the explosion in home crafting and how many crafters are using their hobbies to relieve stress and unleash their creativity, which often spills over into other areas of their lives.

SECTION ONE: A STITCH IN TIME covers the stitching and sewing craft categories, including cross-stitch, macramé, rug hooking, embroidery, knitting, and sewing doll's clothes. Each category includes a list of needed materials, tips on developing your design, time-savers and "add-ons" to make your creation unique.

SECTION TWO: PUT IT ON PAPER covers scrapbooking, photo collages, calligraphy, and paper-making. Each category includes a list of needed materials, tips on developing your design, time-savers and "add-ons" to make your creation unique.

SECTION THREE: BEADING shows how to make jewelry, photo frames, baskets, dolls and other bric-a-brac using plastic, ceramic and wooden beads. Each category includes a list of needed materials, tips on developing your design, time-savers and "add-ons" to make your creation unique.

SECTION FOUR: SILK AND DRIED FLOWERS covers a variety of home decorating ideas using silk and dried flowers for holiday or everyday display. Each category includes a list of needed materials, tips on developing your design, time-savers and "add-ons" to make your creation unique.

SECTION FIVE: PAINTING, STAMPING AND STENCILING shows simple ways to dress up everything from glassware to old shoes with paints, stamps and stencils. Each category includes a list of materials, tips on developing your design, and "add-ons" to make your creation unique.

SECTION SIX: FURNITURE FIXES covers painting, refinishing and upholstering chairs, sofas, ottomans, tables, bookcases, and cabinets to create a new and unique feel at a fraction of the cost of purchasing new furniture. Each category includes a list of needed materials, tips on developing your design, time-savers and "add-ons" to make your creation unique.

INTRODUCTION

Unleashing Your Inner Creativity

Home crafts are enjoying record popularity these days, whether it's creating cute scrapbooks of photos and mementos as thoughtful gifts for birthdays and holidays or sprucing up a ratty-looking chair or cabinet to give it new life. In fact, there are so many choices out there for the new crafter that it can be intimidating just to decide what medium you want to work in. This book aims to take some of that intimidation out of the world of crafting by showing you simple and inexpensive ways to experiment with the major areas in home crafting.

Why do people like to do crafts? There are lots of reasons.

Meg Schneider
123 North Street
Suburbia NY 12345
(555) 222-2222
MegSchneider@myemailaddress.com

Jane Smith, Acquisitions Editor
ABC Publishers
P.O. Box 1111
Big City NY 54321

April 27, 2005

Dear Ms. Smith,

At some point in her life, every woman has felt trapped in a mundane existence and wished for a magical transformation. In the modern age, we seek such magic in cosmetics, clothes shops, and fitness clubs. But in another age, a lucky few had much more potent magic at their disposal: benevolent fairies who bestowed favors upon the deserving.

CINDERELLA is a tale of one such young woman, good-hearted and full of inner beauty but trapped in a life of drudgery and ill-treatment from her vain and cruel stepmother and two stepsisters. She has no means to escape her sorrowful lot until her fairy godmother appears and uses her magic to reveal Cinderella's true beauty and worth to the world. Written with humor and poignancy, CINDERELLA weaves current social issues of class distinction, self-image and self-worth into a timeless fantasy world populated by fallible humans and the supernatural beings who watch over them.

I am an award-winning writer with 17 years' experience in television, radio, newspaper and public relations. My book credits include *Everything Writing a Book Proposal* (Adams Media, May 2005), *Everything Casino Gambling* (Adams Media, September 2004), and *The Birth Order Effect for Couples* (Fair Winds Press, January 2004). At 65,342 words, CINDERELLA is my first novel.

Thank you for your time and consideration. I look forward to hearing from you.

Sincerely,
Meg Schneider

CINDERELLA

Synopsis

Cinderella has had a tough life. Her mother died when she was young, and her adoring father, feeling the child needed a mother, marries a woman with two daughters of her own. Cinderella senses an ominous undercurrent from her stepmother and stepsisters, but she is protected from any overt abuse by her father. Unfortunately, her father dies shortly afterwards, and Cinderella's status in the blended family disintegrates almost immediately to that of indentured servant.

For a long time, Cinderella is forced to do all the household chores for her vain and wicked stepmother and her equally vain and wicked stepsisters. She sleeps in the smallest, barest room in the house, wears the same tattered, dirty clothes day after day, and endures the cruel taunts of the others as she does her never-ending work.

One day, word comes that the king, whose son is of the age to marry, will hold a magnificent ball to introduce the prince to all the maidens of the land. Cinderella desperately wants to attend the ball, but her stepmother relegates her to the role of lady's maid for her stepsisters and points out that, even if she did complete her chores in time to go to the ball, Cinderella has nothing but rags to wear. "What prince would waste his time on a filthy servant girl like you?" the stepmother snipes.

Cinderella watches her stepmother and stepsisters leave for the ball. When they are well away, she breaks down and cries as if her heart would break, trapped and hopeless. Through her sobs, she hears a tiny sound and looks up, astonished to see a twinkling fairy gazing benevolently upon her. The fairy asks Cinderella why she is so unhappy, and when Cinderella explains that she has no fine clothes to wear to the ball and no way to get to the king's palace, the fairy says, "But you shall go to the ball, my child." Then the fairy uses her magic to clad Cinderella in a beautiful gown and exquisite slippers made of glass; a pumpkin and four mice are transformed into a golden carriage, horses and footmen. "The magic will last until midnight," the fairy says. "After that, everything must be the way it was." Cinderella, awed and elated, thanks the fairy and promises to be home before the last stroke of midnight.

At the ball, Cinderella's arrival sets tongues whispering about who she could be, for no one, not even her stepmother and stepsisters, recognizes the downtrodden servant in the lovely young woman. The handsome prince is immediately smitten, and soon he is leading Cinderella across the ballroom floor, ignoring all the other maidens. The evening passes quickly, and it seems but a moment before the clock begins to toll the strokes of midnight. So enchanted is Cinderella that she barely hears the clock, and four strokes have already sounded by the time she remembers the fairy's warning. Frightened of being exposed in front of the prince and her wicked stepfamily, Cinderella runs from the palace. As she flies down the steps, one of her glass slippers falls off. She keeps running, and as the clock registers the final toll of midnight, her fine clothing disappears, replaced by her usual rags, and the spectacular carriage, horses and footmen resume their original forms.

Meanwhile, the prince has found the glass slipper on the palace steps. He doesn't understand why the beautiful girl ran away so abruptly, but he knows he is in love with her, and he resolves to find her. The following morning, he begins a methodical search of the kingdom, stopping at every house and hovel and having every woman he encounters try on the mysterious glass slipper. Eventually, he arrives at Cinderella's home and explains his errand to the stepmother. In turn, the two stepsisters and the stepmother try to jam their substantial feet into the tiny slipper, but it clearly fits none of them. The prince prepares to ride away, but he spots Cinderella behind the house, filling a bucket from the well. The stepmother tries to prevent Cinderella from trying on the slipper, but the prince insists. Cinderella, nervous and not sure what will happen, shyly tries the slipper on. Instantly she is transformed into the beautiful maiden of the ball. The prince gathers her into his arms and declares his undying love, then carries her away to his palace to live happily ever after.

Index